COLLABORATION ECONOMY

"Business in the 21st century is no longer a zero-sum game where the winner takes all. The new leaders will be those who activate and thrive in the global collaboration economy."

—**Yanik Silver**, Founder Maverick1000

"They say content is king, but now and in the future, there's a new king on the block. It's collaboration. If you want to succeed, you must read this book and implement what you learn."

—**Ryan Lee**, RyanLee.com

"The bigger your dream, the more important your team. And the *Collaboration Economy* is all about how you fortify yourself with the right people, JV's, affiliates, and collaborations to rapidly accelerate your success and significance. If you want to reach more people and create more IMPACT, collaboration is the name of the game. This is a must read book!"

—**Todd Durkin**, MA, CSCS Owner, Fitness Quest 10 Lead Training Advisor, Under Armour

"*The Collaboration Economy* is jam packed full of easy-to-apply strategies that will transform your business in today's marketplace."

—**Dan Bradbury**, author of *Confessions of a Millionaire Coach*

"I've known Topher and John through separate business ventures and always had great experiences with their professionalism. When I heard they were collaborating on a book I knew it would be a winner. Sure enough, this book takes you behind the curtain and shows you how they have managed to create alliances with some of the most influential people in their industries. The strategies in this book are priceless!"

—**Forbes Riley**, Award Winning TV Host & Fitness Hall of Fame Inductee *The 2 Billion Dollar Host /* TV Health & Fitness Celebrity

COLLABORATION ECONOMY

*Eliminate the Competition by
Creating Partnership Opportunities*

JOHN SPENCER ELLIS
and TOPHER MORRISON

NEW YORK

COLLABORATION ECONOMY
Eliminate the Competition by Creating Partnership Opportunities

Published in New York, New York, by Morgan James Publishing. Morgan James and The Entrepreneurial Publisher are trademarks of Morgan James, LLC.
www.MorganJamesPublishing.com

The Morgan James Speakers Group can bring authors to your live event. For more information or to book an event visit The Morgan James Speakers Group at www.TheMorganJamesSpeakersGroup.com.

BitLit

A FREE eBook edition is available with the purchase of this print book

CLEARLY PRINT YOUR NAME IN THE BOX ABOVE

Instructions to claim your free eBook edition:
1. Download the BitLit app for Android or iOS
2. Write your name in UPPER CASE in the box
3. Use the BitLit app to submit a photo
4. Download your eBook to any device

ISBN 978-1-61448-983-2 paperback
ISBN 978-1-61448-984-9 eBook
ISBN 978-1-61448-986-3 hardcover
Library of Congress Control Number:
2013951387

Cover Design by:
Rachel Lopez
www.r2cdesign.com

Interior Design by:
Bonnie Bushman
bonnie@caboodlegraphics.com

In an effort to support local communities, raise awareness and funds, Morgan James Publishing donates a percentage of all book sales for the life of each book to Habitat for Humanity Peninsula and Greater Williamsburg.

Get involved today, visit
www.MorganJamesBuilds.com.

Habitat
for Humanity®
Peninsula and
Greater Williamsburg
Building Partner

TABLE OF CONTENTS

ACKNOWLEDGEMENTS

Topher's Acknowledgements

I would like to first acknowledge my co-author John Spencer Ellis. I met john nearly 20 years ago, and we've done several projects together. He has always delivered on what he said he would do. I'm honored to call him a business partner and a friend. Some other people that definitely deserve some credit:

Daniel Priestley, the author of *Become a Key Person of Influence* whose entrepreneurial acumen leaves me humbled every time we speak.

Kevin Harrington, from *ABC's Shark Tank*... thanks for the awesome foreword for this book!

Mandi Foster & Jodi Mclean, I couldn't ask for a better team! I'm blessed to come to work each day and work beside you two!

Anthony Amos, this crazy Australian is like a human Google... he's connected to everyone.

Roger James Hamilton, the creator Wealth Dynamics, and one of the most insightful men I've ever met.

Dan Bradbury, one of the few people in the business coaching world that I think knows what the hell he's talking about.

John Heffron, funniest comedian alive and a great co-author. (I only co-author with Johns…keeps it simple that way)

Peter Rosegarten, the best manager a person could have. I appreciate you more than I ever tell you.

And the most important Collaboration in my life…Kermit & Donna Morrison, married for over 50 years and my source of daily inspiration.

John's Acknowledgements

My list of mentors and people of inspiration is lengthy. I first must thank my wife Kelli who supports all of my crazy ideas, and challenges me with her intelligence each day.

Of course, I need to thank my co-author Topher Morrison. He is funny, ethical, and a great collaboration partner.

Al and Marilyn Sargent are two people who have helped me make the toughest decisions of my life with positive outcomes. I would not have this wonderful life without their influence and guidance.

My incredible staff which supports my network of companies. They are loyal, dedicated and always have my back.

Some influential people in my life, and who have shaped my understanding of business are the following: Tim Ferris, T. Harv Eker, Seth Godin, Gary Vaynerchuk, Malcolm Gladwell, Ryan Lee, Yanik Silver, Brendon Burchard, Chalene Johnson, Debbie Allen, John Assaraf and all cast members of *The Compass*.

A special thanks to members of KBL, The Pack and my fellow fitness entrepreneurs.

Finally, thank you to my mom and dad who keep me balanced, and support my business and entrepreneurial endeavors. My dad was my first entrepreneurial teacher, and my mom taught me the importance of savings and a back-up plan.

FOREWORD

I remember approaching a crowd of people huddled around one man selling a set of knives at the Philadelphia Home Show. His pitch was perfect. He wasn't a salesman; he was an entertainer. The crowd was laughing and the way he used his words created vivid images in the minds of everyone watching.

It was the mid 80s and I had just seen one of the best pitchmen ever. His name was Arnold Morris and he was the presenter of the Ginsu Knives. How he got those knives so sharp, I don't know. I can only guess they were sharpened by his wit. I'll never forget how the audience would laugh as he shouted out his signature lines…

"You can cut this tomato so thin you can read the Sunday paper through it"

"You can slice the tomato so thin it will last you all week"

At the end of his presentation, over half the crowd would pull out twenty dollars to be the proud new owner of a set of Ginsu Knives, and Arnold Morris was the proud new owner of about $200. Not bad for a 15-minute presentation in the 1980s.

Before I could approach him, he had already called around another group of 20 or so people, and he launched back into his pitch with the same jokes, same vegetables and same results. Cha Ching… another $200 went into his back pocket.

I didn't see any more of the home show that day. I stayed there watching him deliver this pitch about 3 times an hour until the end of the day. Finally, as he was packing up what was left of his inventory, which wasn't much, I approached.

"I've been watching you all day long, that's quite a presentation you have there."

"Well when you've been doing it for over 30 years you tend to know what works and stick with what works."

That's when I knew he was a great salesman but a struggling entrepreneur. He had been selling his knives for 30 years the exact same way because it worked. There's an inherent danger in continuing to do something because it works. It keeps you from finding ways to make it work even better.

Be willing to abandon already working methods for even better working methods.

Arnold had been selling knives for nearly 30 years. Considering how hard he worked, how perfected his pitch had become, and how long he had been in the business presenting the knives, I estimated that he had probably earned over $1 million dollars in that 30 year span. Not a bad life. Then he met me.

I realized that if we just videotaped him delivering his pitch and put the presentation on TV he could sell the Ginsu knives in more than one city at a time for more than 8 hours a day. It wasn't my first infomercial, but it was certainly my most successful at that time. We did over $100 million dollars in sales and Arnold had a brand new life.

If you are doing business today the same way you were 5 years ago, then there's a very good chance your sales are down. And if they aren't, just wait. They will be down. The markets have changed. The economy isn't what it used to be. I'm not saying it's worse. I'm saying it's different. Whether or not the economy for you is better or worse will come down to your willingness to reinvent the way you do business. Shake things up. Try new things and innovate, innovate, innovate.

John Spencer Ellis and Topher Morrison are committed to staying ahead of the trends and reinventing how they run their businesses. Both John and Topher have a knack for taking something that works, and finding a way to make it work even better. This is how I've built my career over the years and I would encourage you, as you read through this book, to get rid of your "yeah butt" or "that's not how I've done it in the past" or the "that will never work for me" thinking.

Make Your Business More Efficient Through Technology

The fact of the matter is business is changing. 15 years ago my infomercial sales were all from TV. Television has been very good to me, and I owe well over $4 billion in revenue to my bottom line because of that magical box.

Imagine how I felt when the Internet started gaining exposure? Far too many people in my business thought nothing could replace the 400 lb. gorilla—TV. But I realized that as technology advanced, so must the methods by which I did business. Realizing a change was about to occur, but unaware of how massive that change would be, we started by just adding our websites to the informercial call to action page. As technology advanced, and popularity of the Internet grew, we began hosting our infomercials normally seen on TV onto our websites.

Now, a full 40% – 50% of all our infomercial product sales come from the Internet. If I had looked at the Internet 15 years ago thinking, "but that's not how I sell products" I would have missed out on a multi-billion dollar market. But as a result of my willingness to break the mold, try new strategies—no matter how unproven or scary they were at the time—I now run the largest Internet product website asseenontv.com for products sold by as seen on TV in America.

Nowadays, the camera inside your iPhone is more sophisticated than the $2.5 million dollar studio I had 20 years ago. Technology has made what used to be accessible only to the very wealthy corporations, now easily accessible for the small business owner. In short—Small IS the new Big.

Create Powerful Connections with Key People of Influence

I'm probably best known outside my industry for my appearances on the first 3 seasons of *Shark Tank*. During that time, I made lots of investments. Some were winners, and some were losers, but perhaps the best thing to have come out of *Shark Tank* for me wasn't even the businesses I acquired. It was the connections I made with the other Sharks.

Collaboration Economy is based on the power of creating powerful connections with key people of influence outside of your sphere of influence so that you can expand your reach beyond what you could do alone.

As you read through this book, be open to the idea that no matter how good your business is doing, it can do even better. But that improvement will not happen if you just keep doing business the same way you always have. Be open to try new technologies that can streamline your business, and not just create efficiency. Because the ultimate goal isn't to become more efficient; it's to become more effective. For small business owners, that effectiveness will happen by your ability to make the 'daily grind' part of your business far more efficient so you have the time to do the things that bring in the big bucks.

Lastly, use the information that John and Topher share with you in *Collaboration Economy* to create more rewarding, and higher caliber partnerships. They don't want you to get more joint venture partners. They want you to get BETTER joint venture partners. And the techniques inside *Collaboration Economy* can do just that.

—**Kevin Harrington** from ABC's "Shark Tank"

INTRODUCTION

With all of the talk in the media about how the economy is in dire straits—not just in America, but across the globe—everybody seems to be hurting or living in fear. There is worry, panic and concern about where the economy is heading, and, in turn, how businesses of all sizes will manage.

Yet, from our perspective, it's more about money changing hands, and it being more challenging to track and measure. It's more about the economy evolving and meaning something different. If you take a closer look at the new hands that are accumulating rather than losing wealth, you might realize that we live in a collaboration economy—a new economy where collaboration begets success.

In fact, our ability and opportunity to make money is better (and easier) than it was in the 1970s, '80s, '90s and early 2000s. The way business was done then doesn't work very well for most small businesses today. However, there are several new and effective ways of succeeding in today's economy.

The keys? Collaboration, innovation, exploration.

"*Collaboration Economy*" was written to help you understand:

- How to succeed in today's business climate
- What you can do to evolve your business from the old economy model to the new collaboration economy
- How to work together to work better
- How to find the right partners
- How to make money while making sense of this new economy

While big businesses often complain about the economy, it is small businesses that are the lifeblood of economies around the globe, and the fastest growing sector of companies in the market today. In the United States, the United Kingdom, Australia and other countries, small businesses are working with innovation, new practices and new success stories.

Signs of optimism include:

- Month over month, small businesses continue to report greater optimism and hiring.
- Heading into 2013, 31 percent of small businesses said they planned to add employees while only 3 percent expected to decrease overall employees; more than half expected revenue to increase, according to a recent Bank of America survey.
- From 2005 to 2010, small-business start-ups created an impressive 19.6 million jobs, according to the Small Business Administration.
- Crowdfunder estimates that if Americans shifted just 1 percent of the $30 trillion they hold in long-term

investments to small businesses, the market for business crowdfunding could quickly reach $300 million.

What is a "collaboration economy?"

Just like the name sounds, a collaboration economy involves working together (or collaborating) to boost business (your economy). It is about partnerships, mentorships and connections. It is about realizing that when we work together, we can all work together.

That doesn't mean that just anyone and everyone should be a collaborator with your business. It's important to learn to distinguish between a great business opportunity and one you should pass on, something we'll discuss later.

Essentially, you want to collaborate with the people and the businesses that share your common values and goals, and complement your skills, so you can offer each other mutual support and growth in your respective industries.

Put simply, a collaboration economy is 1 + 1 = 3 (or even more).

THE OLD ECONOMY VS. THE NEW ECONOMY

I t's truly a tale of two economies.

The way it was done, and the way it can be done.

The old versus the new: A dated economy that worked for a short while, and an insightful economy that will work for the long run.

The way it was and the way it is

There is a big difference between the old way business used to be done and the new way business is being done right now. One of the best resources on this topic is a recently published book called "*Entrepreneur Revolution*" by Daniel Priestley. This fantastic book offers great insight with regard to how new entrepreneurs are succeeding.

If you are still doing business the old way, you are probably suffering and struggling. If you are doing business the new way, you still might feel a bit lost or confused sometimes, and this book will help you address just this issue in today's every-changing climate.

The old way in which we used to do business included something called the "net mentality," where we would try to catch anything and everything we could by casting the biggest and widest and farthest net possible. This might have worked when things were simpler and you knew everyone in your neighborhood, everyone in your business district, maybe most everyone in your small town.

This might have worked when there were just three TV channels and limited options for outreach. You would turn the TV on and your choices were ABC, NBC and CBS. But today, there are way more than three channels, and there are also far more than just a few businesses out there that offer the products and the services that your customers might need.

From three stations to a million options

Using the media as an example, there used to be just a few channels broadcasting to millions of people. With the new media, there are millions of channels broadcasting to just a select group of people. Those channels are no longer operated by only by big corporations. They are frequently operated by college kids who found a new and innovative way to communicate with each other.

Likewise, think of all the niche stations that now target niche individuals—the Golf Channel for golf lovers, Nickelodeon for kids, Lifetime for women—and the list goes on and on. These are all great examples of new ways of doing business and reaching out to specific customers, rather than just casting the biggest net possible and hoping to lure something or someone in.

Facebook is another great example. In 2004, Facebook (originally named, TheFacebook) started off as a very small micro-niche product, a way that founder Mark Zuckerberg and his college friends could keep in touch with each other at Harvard. He opened it up to other colleges, but the only people who were allowed to have a Facebook account then were those who had a ".edu" email account, indicating that they were enrolled at a college or university. After it continued to grow in popularity, Zuckerberg and associates eventually opened Facebook up to the public.

As of May 2013, Facebook boasted:

- More than 1.1 billion users
- More than 50 million pages
- 1.13 trillion "likes"
- And more than 10 million Facebook apps

All of that success started with a specific niche. Ironically, today, Facebook is also successful because of the millions of niche fan pages and groups. It came full circle.

If you look at how many channels and ways there are to reach your customers, it's literally infinite. The challenge is that you have to know who your customer is—which is what new business is all about.

Old business used a gigantic net and cast it as far and wide as possible. The new way of doing business is to have your hook and bait it with the exact bait you know your customer wants to bite. When you do that, you are going to be much more focused and much more intentional in your behaviors and your actions.

Likewise, your small business will be much more successful in its efforts.

An idea shared is an idea multiplied

In "*Why Collaboration is Key*," an Entrepreneur.com article written by marketing executive Erika Napoletano, the author discusses the importance of sharing and collaborating on ideas.

She writes: "But ideas alone aren't worth squat. To turn ideas from air into something of value, you first have to admit that you're not special. I'm not special. It's probably the most difficult lesson I've had to learn as an entrepreneur. I'm fallible just like everyone else. The day I stopped thinking all my ideas were brilliant and my business practices above reproach was the day my company started to take off. I realized that, in their infancy, my ideas are just things bouncing around in my noggin like the last three gumballs in a glass globe outside the grocery store."

The article further encourages collaboration with a variety of potential partners and backers and concludes: "So instead of sitting around with your idea, thinking about how pretty it is and how much you love it, start thinking about the people who can help you add some weight to your thinking. The doing: That's the path toward special."

Collaboration is truly key in today's new economy. It's time for "out with the old, and in with the new."

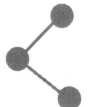

IN SEARCH OF
THE MICRO-NICHE

Just like TV stations specialize in terms of the customers they are trying to reach, it is no longer possible to succeed easily with a niche; you need to have a micro-niche in today's business world.

You can no longer, for example, be a fitness trainer who specializes in general boot camps. Instead, you might be fitness trainer who specializes in boot camps for women or boot camps for a specific sport or boot camps for teens. When you micro-niche to that level of specificity, you immediately know your customer, and where they live, and know how to communicate with them.

In fact, a great way to know whether or not you have a micro-niche is to answer this question:

Do you know where your customers are?

By the way, the answer cannot be "everywhere." Once you know the answer to that question, you probably are on your way to establishing a pretty good micro-niche.

For example, if you run a coaching business specific for female divorcees, can you answer the question, "Where do female divorcees hang out?" Where are they? Would you be able to find them? The answer is "yes," you can find social networking support groups for female divorcees. You can find local meet-up groups online for local female divorcees. You also know that future female divorcees are at law firms—that you can network with attorneys and law firms that specialize in divorce to offer your coaching services for their female clients. These are just a few ways in which you can quickly assess "Who are my customers and where are they?" If you don't have a clear answer, you haven't micro-niched small enough.

Turning off some to turn on success

You have to be okay with the idea and necessity of turning some people off as much as you turn others on to what it is that you are doing. This can be a true challenge for small businesses, but is important as you establish your micro-niche: Know who you are and know who your customers are—and aren't.

One of the greatest measuring tools you can use for your marketing material is to look at your ads and ask yourself, "Would this marketing turn off the people who are NOT in my target market?" If the answer is "no," then your marketing message isn't powerful enough.

The best ad agencies in the world measure the effectiveness of their branding by its level of repulsion to people who are not in their niche. When we refer to "repulsion" or "turning off," we don't mean it in an offensive or negative way. However, if somebody is not in your niche market, they will never want to do business with you and you need to recognize that right off the bat. You will never catch them with your net, so you should simply focus on the potential customers who you can catch—and excite—within your micro-niche.

For example, if "life coaching for female divorcees" was plastered on your website, and you put together ads that drove traffic to your rather feminine website, men who visited your website would likely be turned off by it. They wouldn't want to look at it. That's why you measure the effectiveness of your marketing by the level of this repulsion. If there is no repulsion, there is no attraction.

The mindset of the entrepreneur or business owner plays a big role, since that individual is likely involved at least in some part of the company's marketing and the branding. It's a matter of being okay with people not liking you or what you stand for in the effort and in the pursuit of finding the right group. The smaller group will not only be interested in what you have to say, but is in perfect alignment and harmony with your messaging, your product and your services.

All of the best brands know: **If your marketing isn't strong enough to repel the audience you do not want, it will never be strong enough to attract the audience you do want.**

A great way to look at how this is affecting us in today's economy and market is to watch a sitcom from 20 years ago. Look at the quality of humor and the jokes and how polite they are and how politically correct they are. Then look at the most popular sitcoms that are on TV today and look at how politically incorrect they are and how offensive they often are in their humor, specifically to make sure that they are getting their methods across to their target market.

Sitcoms are a great reflection on how we look at our real-world environment. Today, it is all about being controversial, being vocal and being unapologetic to what it is that your product stands for to your ideal customer. Truly, if somebody is not in your target market, they should not even be tempted with the offer to make the purchase.

Be audacious, not abrasive

Every business that is developing and refining a particular niche while building a business brand needs to walk the fine line between being audacious and abrasive. It is okay to be outlandish, unusual and interesting—you can be direct and opinionated so people know that they can stand behind you and your brand. And if you are milquetoast or a wallflower, how in the world will that ever make anyone want to align with you?

Being audacious is within in the scope of any business' vision, and it can also play a role in your presentation of your perspective. It might be in the branding of the business itself, and it can take on many other forms. You want to avoid becoming a commodity and blending at all costs.

Be outrageous and audacious while you are refining your niche; at this time, you will repel plenty of people so you can attract the smaller, more loyal group who will be with you for a long, long time. However, you don't have to be excessively abrasive or offensive, and it's important to recognize the difference.

Make the news because of the wild vision and advertising you have for your product, not because you've publicly offended an entire culture, gender or age group. Be audacious, not abrasive.

YESTERDAY'S COMPETITORS ARE TODAY'S ALLIES

Stop competing and start collaborating. One of the most unique things about today's economy for business is that your competition has really become your ally.

We'll repeat that again: Today, your competition is your ally.

If you don't believe it, think about how car dealerships place themselves right next to other car dealerships. The reason they do this is

1. It creates group consciousness, helping more people recognize where they can go to buy a car.

2. It creates an environment where, when people walk onto that lot, they are predisposed to want to buy a car.

3. It also accelerates customer service for those who want to shop around. They don't have to spend a lot of money

on gas, drive hundreds of miles and waste hours of their precious time; they can just simply walk across the street to compare products.

If we take that logic and we transfer it to small business owners, the first thing that comes up is competition.

A few years back, one of Topher's clients had a small hypnotherapy practice in Seattle. He called and was concerned because he heard that a national hypnotherapy franchise was moving into the Seattle market and he was afraid that that was going to harm his business.

Topher's response to his client's comments? "Pray that the franchise opens an office in your building because it will only help your business take off," explaining the car dealership analogy. It raises group consciousness, places customers into an environment where they feel it is appropriate to buy, and will allow them to shop around much more efficiently and easily. Within six months, this small business' membership had grown so significantly that the owner needed to add staff and was considering moving into a new office to accommodate all of the additional business.

Interestingly, he received some unexpected feedback in his ongoing customer surveys in which he asked his clients to rate how they enjoyed the service and how they had heard about the business. One of the options to the question "How did you hear about us?" was "TV and radio," and yet this business owner had never taken out a TV or a radio ad. Nevertheless, a majority of the people picked that box, mistaking his company for the national franchise that was spending tens of thousands of dollars every month on advertising.

Open competition online

Another example of how your competition can become your ally the modern way is websites such as 99 Designs. On this particular website, people can request that graphic designers provide design services at a highly discounted rate. The customer simply states what he or she is looking for, the look and the feel of it, and a general budget. Considering this information, site visitors then can work with a series of graphic designers who can create a logo or a design of some sort; the customer only has to pay for the one they love and everyone can immediately see the competition and their work.

A business with an inferior product, inferior service and inferior customer accountability and customer service might not like this type of competition. If you have come up with a very specific niche, the reality is your competition can help you, because most competitors won't have that specific of a micro-niche anyway. Competition can also bring heightened awareness to the work you're doing and the industry you work in.

At 99 Designs, you can have 50 different graphic designers submit their work to you and you can pick the one that you like; the fact that those 49 other designers are competing with the one you pick simply forces all of them to raise their game and provide the best possible customer service.

Ironically, this is a mentality we should probably have as business owners from day one anyway. Imagine how much better your customer service would be if this were your business mindset, if you focused that much more on the quality of product delivery, if every day you went to work thinking that 49 of your competitors were going after the exact same customers that you were targeting at the exact same time and standing directly beside you or your sales rep. If more businesses used this thought process, they would be more prepared, have better products and deliver far better customer service.

Other great examples of competition becoming a great ally:

In Orange County, California, there is a street called State College and it is named after the state college—Cal State Fullerton. On this street, there are no less than 30 tile and marble stores located together side-by-side on each side of the street for as far as the eye can see. Why? It's all designed for the convenience of the customer. What is perhaps even more ironic is that some of the larger stores are frequently the suppliers for some of the smaller stores, because they have more buying power. Yet, the margins are solid enough such that every business can win—and win together. In some cases, if one store is out of a particular product, the business owners have developed an alliance with another tile and marble store on the same street so that they can still fulfill all of their orders. The stores both win, and, of course, the customer definitely wins as well.

Another successful online business, Elance.com, is a website for freelancers that allows you to hire someone to perform a particular task for you, whether it's writing, administrative tasks, legal work, website design or computer programming. For example, if you want someone to write a press release for your business, you can post the project online and state your budget and the project's overall parameters. If you would like to compare two different styles—or perhaps even three or four—you can hire three or four independent contractors through Elance to each write a press release on the same topic, and then you can choose which writing style works best for your business and use that person for future projects. It's an amazing example of competition in action.

Your competition is your ally.

FRICTIONLESS
TRANSACTIONS

We live in a society where we want to get everything immediately and we are looking for the ultimate in convenience. This isn't just an American thing, although we are likely the leaders of the pack. Everywhere you go, people are looking for a fast solution and a convenient way to do anything and everything.

We are on the go, in a rush, waiting impatiently.

The PayPal phenomenon in frictionless transactions
We think of it as the PayPal phenomenon. By helping small business owners that couldn't otherwise get a merchant account to accept credit cards, PayPal has created what we call frictionless transactions.

A frictionless transaction is essentially the ability to make your product or your service so easy to purchase that the consumer doesn't even have to pull out their wallet to give you their money or their credit card.

It's all about convenience, convenience, convenience.

Consider any step that a customer has to take to purchase from you. The company that has probably mastered this the best and the earliest was Amazon.com with its 1-click purchase process. Do you remember the first time you went to buy a book or something else through Amazon and saw the "1-click to purchase" icon? The company instantly responds, "Congratulations, you've purchased the book. It will be sent to your home address." Once your address and payment information are set up, Amazon keeps all of that information readily available so whenever you want to buy something, you don't have to locate your credit card, enter the information and wait. It's a great frictionless transaction.

If you are asking, "How can I become as efficient at selling my product or service as Amazon.com?" then you are definitely headed in the right direction.

Always ask yourself if there is a way to simplify, expedite and streamline the process.

An apple a day makes money

Here's another example of how frictionless transactions make buying attractive: Apple founder Steve Jobs had this crazy notion that if he could make buying music simple, easy and affordable, people would be willing to pay for something which many were already getting for free through Napster and other downloading piracy programs. He created iTunes. iTunes is a perfect example of how you can buy things with a completely frictionless transaction.

Created in 2003, by February 2013, the iTunes store had sold more than 25 billion songs worldwide.

The same goes with apps: I'm looking on my iPhone; I see an app I want to buy; I click to buy it. Apple already has all of my payments information stored and the deal is done. If you question the power of frictionless transaction, at the time of this printing Apple Inc. has the largest collection of credit cards in the world.

The more convenient something is, the easier it is to buy. Likewise, if you can avoid reminding someone about what it costs by storing their payment information, you make the buying experience that much more enjoyable.

Less friction, more convenience

As the power and convenience of frictionless transactions continue to grow over the next few years, credit cards will become virtually unnecessary. Cash will become a thing of the past because we will be able to purchase everything through retina scans, fingerprints and personal pin codes.

It's happening already. When you walk into your local Starbucks, you don't need to have any cash or credit cards on you. You simply pull out your smart phone (which immediately recognizes that you're in Starbucks), select Passbook option, and all of a sudden your bar code reader is there and you can buy your coffee without ever having to deal with any currency. Your morning half-caf skinny latte tastes better than ever.

Another thing that is fascinating and proof positive this is the way of the future, is the fact that iTunes and Amazon account for nearly half of every single transaction that takes place on the Internet thanks to their convenient user interface which provides tremendous ease of use. Early adopters of frictionless transactions have made a lot of money and won over millions of fans.

Frictionless transactions and your business

As you develop your empire, as your grow your tribe, as you go from thinking about entrepreneurship to driving a successful and happy business, you need to continually ask yourself, "Where are my customers?" Your customers are using iTunes and Amazon and, in some cases and to a lesser degree, e-Bay. When and if possible, your product or services should be sold through these reliable institutions on the web. Your customers will appreciate the convenience and you will appreciate the incremental business. The process is simple, fast and free.

The whole notion of small businesses even having to have merchant accounts is quickly becoming obsolete, or at least far less important:

- By aligning yourself with companies like Amazon.com, iTunes and so many others, you will be able to run your business and take transactions.
- Although you will split revenues or pay commissions with Amazon, iTunes or eBay, the exposure you will get and the selling power that you will have will far outweigh the additional commissions or revenue shares you pay these companies.
- If you are designing your own website and setting up your own company, how can you create frictionless transactions just like these successful businesses? If, for example, you are a restaurant and you have a repeat customer, technology is such today that there is no

reason whatsoever that you should ever need to ask them for their credit card when they return a second, a third, a fourth and a fifth time. In fact, if you could do this with your restaurant, the likelihood of repeat business would increase due to the ease and the simplicity that you have created in the buying process. If you run a small garage doing repairs, the moment a customer comes back a second time—and if they've already provided you payment—there is no reason why you should have to ask them for payment details a second time. The notion of having to ask the customer for their payment information more than once is a business model pointing you toward the past.

- Taking repeat payments is inconvenient for your business. There are other secondary aspects of this that need to be considered as well. Every time you have to ask your customer for payment information, they recognize that money is leaving their bank, their account, their wallet or their purse. But if you can, at least at a subconscious level, eliminate the financial implications of the transaction to where the customer can focus more on the product benefits, they are more likely to seek more products and seek more benefits. Whenever possible, eliminate any need to ask for payment ongoing.

- Successful and smart small business owners today are focusing on how they can get their products or services into companies which have already established and created the best frictionless transactions. Create opportunities for ongoing payments and frictionless transactions and you will realize success with sales, saving time and convenience.

Topher regularly puts together a variety of events where his team identifies KPIs, or Key Persons of Influence. Every KPI at an event receives a QR code, which is located on the back of their nametag at the seminar. These key influencers are also asked if they would like to upgrade to a silver or gold ticket. If they are interested, all we have to do is scan their QR code and the payment is made and the upgrade is complete—it's that simple and that effective.

Likewise, when these attendees take a look at various vendors' products and services, if they see something they want to purchase, rather than having to buy things with their credit card, they simply have to show their name tag, have their QR code scanned and we instantly take their payment—no need for a credit card or cash. Receipts are automatically emailed to them and they walk out with their product, which involves zero friction.

The cruise ship industry also does a terrific job of this—they have absolutely mastered frictionless transactions. If you have not been a cruise recently, here is a quick snapshot of how it works. All passengers have a credit card on file and they will check that credit card to make sure that it can handle what it is that they want you to do on any side trips and what the cruise line wants you to enjoy throughout your voyage. In exchange, the cruise ship will give you what is called a "Cruise and Carry Card" to serve two purposes:

- It is your identification while you are on the ship for safety, for calls or immigration, and as you go in and out of the places that you visit while on your cruise.
- It also allows you to charge your extra cocktails. It allows you to buy things in the gift shop. It allows you to upgrade to different services. You can use it to pay for

short excursions if you haven't paid for them in advance. Essentially, it allows you to enjoy—and spend—more.

The real benefit here is that once you're on the ship, at some level, you dissociate your actions with paying more money. You wouldn't think it would happen after being on multiple cruises over a period of years, but, in fact, it does happen to everyone at least to some degree. The result is that if a person purchases a cruise with a value of $1,000, it is very likely that they will double that amount in incidentals throughout the time they are on the ship and the cruise ship industry knows this for certain.

As an example, when Carnival Cruise, one of the preeminent cruise lines in the world, was first getting started, they did not have a lot of money for advertising, but they would trade the ads in major metropolitan newspapers in exchange for allowing newspaper executives to come on the ship for free. It worked out well for everyone. Carnival got free advertising and it allowed them to grow their business. The executives got on the ship with their families at no cost. Carnival knew something above and beyond this: They knew that these executives and their family members, once on the ship, would have their Cruise and Carry Card and that they would not factor in the whole amount until the end of the cruise when the bill arrived and by that time, it's too late.

Frictionless transactions will drive customers and drive business: How can you reduce friction to zero within your small business?

TURNING THE SALES MODEL UPSIDE DOWN

T he old small business sales model was very simple: If you wanted something, you had to pay for it and then you would get it. It makes perfect sense.

The new sales model, however, is completely the opposite. It starts with take it, you can have it for free and if you like it, then you can pay me for it.

That makes no sense to us as entrepreneurs, and yet we both recognize that the way of doing business is constantly changing.

You can resist and lose, or you can cooperate and flourish. The more you fixate on the past, you more you won't face the future and will suffer the consequences when it comes to your business. No matter how much you fight and kick and scream, in the end, you're going to have to give the new sales model a chance: Give your product or service away and then let people pay for it if they like it. Times are changing, and so, too, are successful small business practices. What can you give away for free and still benefit if people pay for it or not? Who can you collaborate with to provide a product or service for free?

If you'd like more information, statistics and advice on this new notion of business, check out a great book called "*Free*" by Chris Anderson; the book will help you recognize and realize the benefits for giving away your products and services for free.

Why free?

One of the reasons this has happened is that information is no longer valued the way it used to be.

The information age is dead—it gave up the ghost around the year 2010, although it started fading around 2000. Why do people no longer value information the way they used to? Take a look at a great example: 30 years ago, if you wanted to get a cassette tape program on how to set goals, you would have to spend at least $795 for that very program, but now all of that information is readily available online for free, so there is truly no need to pay for a cassette tape or a CD or a download on how to set goals (unless you really, really want to).

If you look at today's youth, they don't have a notion about limited resources like most of us did 20, 30 or 50 years ago. They have a completely different mindset and recognize that they can get much of what they want for free online. They probably don't even know what a cassette tape is!

If you wanted to learn to play the guitar 30 years ago, the scenario might go something like this:

- You would first go to your parents and tell them you wanted to learn how to play the guitar.
- They would probably say "no" or at least ask many questions. Then they might still say "no."
- After six months of badgering and proving how interested you were to your parents, they might relent, buying you the cheapest guitar available on the market.
- They would find you a guitar instructor and then have to take you to that person's house, sit around and wait for an hour while the instructor taught you chord progressions and then you would go home. You probably wouldn't practice much until the next week—about an hour before your lesson.
- And the cycle would repeat: For guitar lessons or just about anything else.

In this scenario, your skill level at playing guitar would be solely dependent upon your parents' level of generosity and taking you to this music instructor's home each week (plus your willingness to practice).

Today? If a kid wants to learn how to play a guitar, all they have to do is go to YouTube, type in what song they want to learn how to play, and there is an entire instruction and tutorial where they can look at the guitar and watch the person on the screen moving their fingers in just the way that they need to move them. With this method, anyone can learn the songs they want to play at no charge and in a short period of time. If the instructor knows how to collaborate with YouTube effectively, his or her lessons will be complete yet offer an incentive to gain more skill at "the official training site" where students can learn advanced chord progressions for $27 per month.

Kids today do not value information the way they did a generation ago because it's free to them. This is creating a culture throughout our entire society where people are no longer willing to pay for information.

What are they willing to pay for?

- Experience and implementation
- Good service
- Something they can't get anywhere else

If you sell information, your business has become a commodity. Within any market, the moment that your product or service has become a commodity, there is only one determining factor—price. Consumers will almost always go with the cheapest option.

If you are reading this book, however, you likely don't want to be selling your product for the cheapest possible price. You want to find a way that you can charge a premium price.

How is that possible? You have to accept this new way of doing business, which is to provide some free information, so much so that your target audience really likes it and then will be willing to pay for it.

By this point, most business owners will have already asked themselves, "How can this happen?" The smarter question is WHEN will this happen?

The Zero Moment of Truth

It happens at the ZMOT.

Jim Lecinski, the Managing Director of U.S. Sales & Service for Google, has written an amazing book on this subject, and yes… it's free! You can find it here: zeromomentoftruth.com

ZMOT stands for *Zero Moment of Truth.*

Lecinski and the team and Google have determined that you have to provide your prospective customer with **as much free information as you can possibly deliver** before they will feel comfortable paying you. According to Daniel Priestly, the author of "*The Entrepreneur Revolution,*" you must provide approximately seven hours of quality content before trying to request a financial transaction.

This notion leads into a whole new type of commerce—one called "products for prospects"—when you no longer sell your product for cash, you simply sell your product for a prospect. You win your audience's trust, you earn their respect and then after seven hours of providing them free content, they are willing to pay you in return.

If you resist this notion, you will struggle in the new economy.

If you accept it, you will get creative and start asking yourself, "How can I provide seven hours of awesome content for my prospects so before they walk into my door they already have the predisposition of wanting to buy from me?"

For example:

- If you are an attorney, how can you create seven hours of great legal information that is still approved through compliance and legal for you to provide for free?

- If you are a dentist, how can you provide somebody with seven hours of great advice and great information before they have to get their teeth cleaned?

- If you are a financial advisor, how can you offer seven hours of great financial advice that will keep potential clients coming back for more?

- If you are a life coach, how can you offer seven hours of free inspiration that will entice prospective clients?

- If you own a small garage, how can you provide someone seven hours of great content so they know you, like you and trust you and will come back as a paying customer?

One of the ways to do that—and there are hundreds out there, if not thousands—is via YouTube. YouTube is a great way for you to become your own television producer, director and star.

Provided you have taken the time to learn how to speak effectively on camera, you should be able to create seven hours of great informational content that people can locate online and get the exposure they need to your product or service for a very low cost. You can also provide that same content in a book. You can provide that content in a download. It's all about how you can flood your prospective customer with so much information that they feel that you are THE expert.

Money for nothing?

The biggest concern small business owners have when thinking about giving away seven hours of free content and information is, "How can I provide seven hours of content, but not give them the real content that they need to purchase to get the real thing?"

You want to give potential customers your best content up front.

Why? Because it's just information; a bunch of ideas. It will be worth your while. Giving your second or third best information for free will give the illusion that your products or services are only that good.

Here's a great example of how we do not value information, but how we do value great service:

You can go down to any bookstore or visit Amazon.com and you can pay $30 to get a recipe book from Jamie Oliver that has all of his greatest recipes that made him famous. OR you can go to a restaurant and pay somebody who is a Jamie Oliver certified chef and will pay far more for only one of those meals provided inside the recipe book.

The same goes with Wolfgang Puck and Gordon Ramsey. We can buy all of their information at an inexpensive price, but yet we will still pay hundreds of dollars to have that person cook for us just once.

How can you become the Jamie Oliver, the Gordon Ramsey or the Wolfgang Puck of your business? You can become your own celebrity.

HOW TO BE A CELEBRITY

Believe it or not, anyone can become a celebrity. Whether you become the Wolfgang Puck, Kobe Bryant, Angelina Jolie or Oprah Winfrey of your industry is entirely up to you.

The beauty about being a celebrity in your niche is that you can go to all of the fancy restaurants in Hollywood and go through the world's top airports and the paparazzi won't bother you. However, when you do any online or in-person events within your niche after you have successfully branded yourself as this expert, people will want to take their photo with you. They want to hear what you have to say. They will want to know how you can help them, or perhaps how they can help you or hear all about your next big project.

Becoming a celebrity expert, guru, *Key Person of Influence* or leader gives you the chance to share your expertise on a larger scale.

Having that clout is a good thing, even though many people just starting out are reluctant to become that person. However, the good news is there is also a starring role for someone just like that and it is called "the reluctant hero."

The reluctant celebrity hero

If you are a reluctant hero, your situation may be kind of like this: You have built a brand, have built your tribe and you have a following, for a lack of a better word. The people who follow you do so because they like what it is that you do along with who you are.

Your response might be something like this: "I found this problem and I know you're hurting and no one else would step up to do it, so I'm going to do it. I'm going to lead the charge and I will pull us out of this ditch. I just need you to follow me and trust me and I will get you through this storm."

If you are somewhat reluctant to have this expert, guru, leader authority role, you can play upon that in the form of the reluctant hero and it works beautifully. You just have to decide what role it is that you want to play while being authentic. You can do both.

There is a delicate balance to maintain: As you become this authority, this expert, this leader, the person who is going to lead the charge, you need to do something that stands out with audacity and fearlessness. Yet, you also must have certain attributes and qualities that are similar enough to the people who you want to appeal so that they feel related or connected to you in some way. If you are on a pedestal—whether you put yourself there or others did so or through some combination—you might feel out of touch, which can make it difficult for people to relate to you, even if they admire who you are and what you have to offer.

So the question is: How can you establish yourself as an expert, a noted authority and someone who can lead the charge while having the proper attributes that are in sync and in alignment with the people you want to attract? Think about how this might work in your life and your chosen industry.

Experience and environment

The key word we've been speaking about here is experience; providing and creating a wonderful experience for your customer versus just giving them information. One of the biggest myths that self-help gurus have been perpetuating for the past 30 years is the notion that you, as a human being, are not affected or are somehow immune to your surroundings. It is a conscious choice or a subconscious choice for you to determine how you feel at any given time—the notion of cause and effect.

On one hand, when you are speaking with somebody who may be in the victim role, someone who tends to blame everyone and everything for their problems, talking about being the cause in their life versus being the effect of their life is probably a healthy conversation to have, but self-help gurus have taken it too far. They've taken it to a point where many people are now becoming blind to reality and saying their environment doesn't make a difference. If you don't think your environment affects you, why do you lower your voice when you're in a funeral home or a library? Why would you feel it's okay to scream and shout when you go to a sporting event or concert? Our environment impacts us. Our response to the environment determines our behaviors.

In the world of entrepreneurship, the behavior you want your customers to have is one where they purchase your product or your service, so the question then immediately becomes "How can you create the environment necessary to determine the behavior of everybody?"

For example, the environment within Facebook is one where you go there to have everything delivered for free. You never log onto Facebook with your wallet and your credit card in your hand thinking, "What will I be able to buy today on Facebook?" The environment is all about being free, and yet we see thousands of entrepreneurs every day wasting thousands of dollars on Facebook, advertising things on Facebook that they are trying to sell. This is, overall, a mistake. While there are always exceptions to every rule, the majority of people are losing money hand over fist when they pay for ads to simply sell somebody something.

Compare that, on the other hand, to Amazon.com, which has the exact opposite environment. With Amazon.com, you go there specifically for one reason and that is to purchase stuff—that is their environment. Every single person who visits Amazon.com has their metaphorical wallet in their hands and they are ready to purchase something. You rarely log on Amazon.com to window shop. You go there because you know you want to buy something.

So what is the environment that you've created in your business? What environment do you want and need to create in your business? Take some time to assess if you have the appropriate business environment that will create interest, sales and ongoing business.

As we discussed earlier, car dealerships often locate their dealerships right next to other car dealerships—simply because it creates an environment where people want to buy.

As the entrepreneur of the future, it is your job to be conscious of the environment you create on the Internet. It is your job to be conscious of the environment you create when a potential customer walks into your office if you have one. It is your responsibility to be aware of and consciously choose what type of environment your customers are in moment by moment every time they are exposed to your business. This awareness can change the shape, trajectory and overall success of your business.

AFFILIATE SYSTEMS

I f you want to increase and multiply revenue in your business without having to add any additional marketing costs, while ensuring that you are capitalizing and maximizing your ability to get and follow up on referrals, then affiliate systems are the next key in today's collaboration economy.

If you are in a service business where you provide your customers something intangible, which they can't enjoy unless they hire you, then a minimum of 40% of your business should always come through referrals. In the old way of doing business, referrals were an arduous process: You would have to reach out to each of your customers, ask them if they were happy, and then if they responded positively, you would have to ask them if they knew of anybody who could benefit from your services.

At that point, there may have been an awkward pause; no matter how much they liked your product or service, the individual may or may not have felt comfortable with this question and they may have hemmed and hawed and left you without any good referrals. Generally, this was a very clumsy, cumbersome process.

All about affiliate marketing

In the new business model, thanks to today's technology, there is even a new term to describe how to automate your referral system—it's all about affiliate marketing.

Affiliate marketing was made most successful by one of the companies we keep referring to in this business because they've done such an amazing job, Amazon.com. The way Amazon.com grew so rapidly and so quickly is because they created an affiliate program where anyone—you, me, it doesn't matter as long as we have an email address and a computer—could sign on as an affiliate, receive a specialized link to every single product in the Amazon warehouse, post that on a personal website, and if anyone else chose to buy that product through this vocalization of Amazon, you would receive a small percentage of the sales you were directly responsible for influencing.

How to make an affiliate program work for you

It is important to address how affiliate programs can work for you even when you're not working. You shouldn't have to be constantly working on affiliates and referrals in the new economy.

In general, there are three types of people who could be a potential affiliate for you and your business:

- **Promoters:** These are the people who will really give your business a boost. They think what you have to offer is amazing and they are more than happy to promote it on their website, through social media channels, to friends and family, to anyone they meet. The more promoters you have, the better. All you need to do is reward them and thank them and send them on their way; they will be happy to do the rest and publicize your product or service to anyone and everyone. A promoter is really what you want all of your customers to ultimately become. A promoter will take the reins out of your hands and will willingly and eagerly go out and tell people about your products or your services, not because of the commission, but because of the amazing benefits they receive and the outstanding follow-up support that they get from you. Every business owner should be constantly thinking about creating more promoters.

- **Customers:** A customer is someone who has purchased your products or services and they are happy with the purchase. This group would be thrilled to tell people about these products and services, but only when those people ask. They're not inclined to go out of their way to promote your products or services. They will if you hassle them enough, if you constantly call them and email them and remind them over and over. However, you could end up spending a lot of time and energy trying to encourage customers to send out marketing on your behalf. If they do it at all, it's going to be halfhearted, template-driven communication, and it's not going to speak to their core audience the way it needs to.

- **Sleepers:** When you hear someone complain about having to babysit the people who are signed up as an affiliate, this is the group they're talking about. A sleeper is someone who has purchased your product or service, has agreed to fill out or click the affiliate link and sign up, but then finds that promoting your system or your service is far too time-consuming. As a result, they never do anything with it. It is actually pretty easy to become a sleeper for many of the companies you set up affiliate links with. Why? Because they never do anything to keep in touch with you; they may have an affiliate program, but not a very effective one. At the end of the day, if you can make a 10, 20 or a 50% commission selling somebody else's product for the same amount of work that it takes to sell your own products and services for 100% of that commission, you will naturally work on your own. That is a common mentality in this business. All of this means that you need to help sleeper affiliates realize that the 20-50% commission that they might receive on your product is a better deal for them than 100% of the sales on their own product or service. You can do this.

Rather than focus your energy and time on reminding customers to send out referral marketing for you, you would be better off spending that same time rewarding those customers, keeping in touch with them and giving them the most remarkable customer service you could possible imagine.

Following is a great example of just that: Daniel Priestley, an entrepreneur, author and speaker, regularly rents out a night club, restaurant or a pub to have what he calls an "Affiliate

Night." During these events, he brings all of his key affiliates—the promoters and the customers—out to just enjoy company and develop more connections.

The two of us, John and Topher, have a great affiliate relationship with each other. We happily refer people to each other's companies not because of the commissions we get—which we don't even take—but because we both believe so fully in the other person's products and services that we go out of our way to encourage people to reach out to the other one and do business with them. If you want to make your customers your promoters, seek ways to make them your friends. Build up that trust, build up that bond and create that friendship.

Both sides of the affiliate marketing coin

There are two sides to the affiliate network business. If you think about it, being an affiliate or offering an affiliate program is really the essence of the collaboration economy, because without this collaboration, neither the individual nor the company can reach their full potential and maximize their earnings potential. Affiliate marketing is truly the collaborative economy in action, which is one of the reasons we are such strong believers in affiliate networks.

In truth, when done really well, affiliate commissions alone can create more revenue than most full-time professions today.

As you contemplate how you will collaborate in this economy using affiliate programs, there are two different things you can think of:

1. If you have a product or a service that you want to better monetize and increase word-of-mouth and exposure primarily online, then you can offer an affiliate

program—in other words, a commission based on performance—for those who promote and then sell your product. If this is your model, then affiliate marketing is something that you should seriously consider.

2. The other perspective is that you can promote and sell other people's products and services. With this scenario, one question that always comes up is this: How do I know that I'm getting paid in an honest way for the work that I have done or the sales I have created for Company XYZ that offers this widget? How do I know that my $500 commission is accurate?

First, this all depends who you are working with, and you have to remember that not everyone has the same ethical standards. Further, in reality, there are a very few reputable companies and you can think of them in terms of being Switzerland—the neutral countries. These companies are the Switzerland of electronic commerce on the Internet, and what they do is they act as an intermediary—a third party, who oversees the transactions, ensures that the proper compensation and payout is done and that the tracking is done properly. These companies are extremely ethical about payments and commissions and can reduce any concerns.

The best in affiliate programs

In particular, there are three great companies to build your affiliate relationships. With these companies, you can create a product or service and make it available through their network, or you can promote and sell products and services that other people have made available on their network to make a commission.

1. A good choice is Commission Junction, often known as CJ for short. A well-established organization, Commission Junction has a great reputation and the company offers a wide array of products and services that are sold through electronic means. In addition, Commission Junction allows you to sell both physical (something that could be shipped or consumed) and non-physical (an eBook, online learning course, MP3 download or online education) products and services.

2. LinkShare is very similar to Commission Junction. LinkShare offers the opportunity to promote or sell both physical and digital products, and is also well established and reputable. We have used both options for affiliate marketing programs.

3. ClickBank only sells digital products and services. If you decide to be an affiliate of ClickBank and you want to promote your products and services, you will only be promoting digital products. Their reason for doing this? Likely, it has something to do with fewer returns, less hassle, ease of reviewing the products before they are accepted into the ClickBank network and so on. In addition, ClickBank becomes your shopping cart. Every transaction actually goes through them. You don't have to cut a check if you are the person providing the service. You do not have to cut a check to the people who are selling your products. It all goes through ClickBank first. The person who made the sale for you as an affiliate gets paid immediately and the remainder of the money goes into your account. ClickBank is the liaison. They are the system and the

intermediary bank, which allows all of this to take place very painlessly.

With all of these organizations, if you are selling your product or service, you will have a built-in army of people who are ready, willing and able to promote your products or service.

For instance, let's say that you have a coaching program to help real estate agents, and it's a digital product with 10 hours of audio, five hours of video, and a 100-page PDF manual that you've created to help real estate agents realize their full potential and double their income within the next 12 months in any market.

That's your angle. That is your pitch. You take it to ClickBank. Assume that they approve the product to be put into the ClickBank network. As soon as it's approved and live, their army of affiliates is made aware or has the opportunity to review your new product. Think for just a moment about how much you could sell on your own—one person, one website, with a single person's effort. Now think about that multiplied times literally thousands of people who really understand Internet marketing. Does it really matter if you are giving away 50% of the retail price of your product if you have even 500 people selling it for you? It's digital. Does it really matter?

Think about the multiplicity of this. It's leveraging your time, leveraging your effort, and it's leveraging other people's talents and opportunities. All of this is incredibly important in the collaboration economy and in the way the world works today.

You can use all of the affiliate networks if you choose, unless there is some sort of conflict of interest in any of their rules and regulations. If we had to recommend just one, ClickBank is our choice, unless you have a physical product to sell. It is the simplest, most streamlined, most widely recognized and most accepted by Internet marketers and affiliate marketers throughout the world.

NOTE: If you have, or want, your own shopping cart to sell products and services from your own website, we suggest 1ShoppingCart or Infusionsoft for your affiliate program. This allows you to have people promote your programs and earn commissions and puts you completely in control. There are many others, but these top rated. Research and determine the best fit based on your needs and budget.

How much money will I make?

The question that always comes up when it comes to affiliate marketing is:

How much money or what percentage will I make promoting another person's product?

OR

If I am offering my product to another person, how much money do I have to give away to the person who really helps facilitate the sale?

The answer is: It varies.

The commission earned varies based on several key points: Is the product or service physical or digital? A physical product has greater inherent costs. You have to build the physical product. You have to ship the physical product. If there is a return process, there are always costs involved with a return of a physical product. Because of those inherent increased costs with a physical product, the commission earned and the commission paid on the sale of a physical product will generally be less than with digital products.

A digital product has a lower cost of entry. It really has no cost other than continual access to the people who want to purchase and gain access to this digital product or service. Because the person who has created a digital product or service at lower cost, they can pass that cost savings on to you in the form of higher commissions paid to the affiliate.

With a physical product, commissions can range from 3% to 20% on average, although there are several variables at play. A digital product will have a commission ranging from 25% up to 100% commission.

You might be wondering, "How is it possible that I could earn a 100% on a digital product? Why would any business owner ever give away 100% of their profits?"

It's a great question and there is a very logical answer to that and it relates to what is called the back end. For example, if you offer a coaching or mentoring program online and it costs $100 through a company such as ClickBank, they will give you 100% or $100 of that sale. However, there is also an upsale on the back end or else they have a method of keeping people involved with the expectation of future sales, so they give 100% on the front end, because they know the upside of the back end sales far exceeds the $100 and also the 100% they gave you as the affiliate. For you as an affiliate, however, that $100 is certainly worth your time and effort. Once you get an affiliate program going, while there is still a little work and promotion involved, this is by far the best method of making passive income. As an affiliate, you have no support issues, customer service emails or calls and no product development or maintenance challenges.

As you are developing your business or developing your products or service, think about what products you could use as an add-on from these networks to earn a commission in conjunction with the sale of your existing products or service, or which of your products or services you might make available to these networks so that other people can help sell it for you, allowing you to increase your reach, broaden your brand and make more total sales.

Despite the fact that you are giving away a good chunk of the overall sales and commission for your product, in the end your total sales and total revenue should increase dramatically.

If you offer it, will they come?

When you become an affiliate or when you sell a product on an affiliate site, you might think that once your product is approved and uploaded, it will immediately turn into "*The Field of Dreams*," where the business simply comes out of thin air and your product just starts selling itself automatically. In reality, you need to continue to take control of your own destiny and your own success.

The following tips will help you even after you've uploaded your product or service to an affiliate website:

- Take advantage of the tools some of these sites offer: ads, sales copy, case studies, calls to action and so on. You can use many of these on your own website to further promote your product. Generally, you can customize colors and fonts to suit your business.

- Think about seasonal promotional opportunities. For example, if you are doing a blog post on your website about getting in shape for the holidays and you are promoting a weight loss product, then the weight loss company you are an affiliate for may have a seasonal ad that will pop up with a code on your website. Some of them will change automatically because the code is being pulled from a central server, so they will push the ad to you, which is embedded on your site with an updated image based on the current season. In this case, all you have to do is enjoy the incremental sales and success that comes from this option.

Again, the best of the best when it comes to this strategy is Amazon. As an affiliate of Amazon, you can sell anything from books to solar-powered backpacks to Mac computers, and they will provide you with links, text, sales copy, different colors and different sized images—some that are static and some that are dynamic. Amazon makes it easy for you. The important thing is to have the right image that fits the flow of your website, newsletter, blog, social media post or whatever it is that you are working on.

When it comes to colors and consistency, there are two options:

1. You can carefully ensure that any ads or promotions will flow with the structure and colors of your website.
2. The other is to use colors and ads that are in stark contrast with your site, so that they really pop out.

Next time you visit Facebook, look at the ads that pop up because they are deemed relevant to your likes and dislikes. (That's why you filled out all of that personal data on Facebook).

If you are wondering how they know which ads might interest you, they are collecting data on you, otherwise known as data mining, so that the ads are relevant to your personal preferences and sometimes even to what you "like" on your Facebook feed that day.

Notice which of the ads stick out. What colors stick out? Generally, it is the contrasting ads. If the colors of the ads are very similar to the colors and design of Facebook, they will tend to look too much like the architecture of Facebook itself, and they got lost. The look and feel of your online ads is a personal preference that you can play around with as you dive deeper into affiliate marketing.

In addition, it is always important to do some testing when it comes to offering affiliate products on your website. For instance, you may have two ads that are exactly the same, except one is yellow and one is blue, and you can drop a very simple code in there for testing purposes. ClickBank allows you to use such codes for tracking; if the yellow ad pulls twice as much business and interest as the blue one, then get rid of the blue and use the yellow on the other page as well. It's that simple and that effective and definitely worth your time.

We have a friend named Sam Bakhtiar who likes to say, "You can't expect what you don't inspect." So if you do not inspect what's happening in your affiliate programs, if you don't test your ads and if you do not compare A to B, then you won't know which way to flip the switch to where you can double the return for your efforts.

PERSONAL BRANDING

Branding is the fun, cool part of the collaboration economy. The cool thing about branding is that it is—and always will be—far stronger than any economic climate. When the economy is good, if you have branded yourself well, you should be set for a great career; if the economy is bad and you have branded yourself well, you're going to be able to withstand the tough times and excel when other small businesses will likely be struggling.

First off, it is important to understand the difference between personal branding and personal marketing with the help of a few common terms.

1. **Sales:** What you do to get people to give you money. It's that simple. Anytime you're having a conversation with someone and you want him or her to purchase something

from you, you are clearly in the sales mode. A lot of people think that they have marketing copy designed to get visitors to buy something. That's not marketing copy, that's sales copy, and there is a difference.

2. **Marketing:** What you do to get people to know who you are. It's about getting that message out there to the right people at the right place at the right time. Quite often, people think that when you are selling, you are also marketing, but when you're marketing you may not be selling. So sales is one aspect, and then a bigger aspect that includes all of selling is marketing, and then beyond that you have branding.

3. **Branding:** The emotional connection that people associate with you and their problems/solutions. It is the first and foremost powerful thing out there for small businesses and if it's done correctly, branding will allow you to compete with big business.

The key to effective branding is to realize that there's no possible way that you cannot brand yourself. Everything you do in life is about developing your brand.

Branding is more than just logos

A lot of people think that branding is your logo. In fact, a logo is just a tiny, tiny part of your overall brand. If branding were just a logo, then Richard Branson wouldn't be a popular person. Just that big "V" with the word "Virgin" would be a popular thing. A personal brand goes way beyond that.

We have both read almost every book written about, or written by, Sir Richard Branson. He tells a story about when he was going through the intellectual properties process, including the branding and logo design and the naming rights of Virgin. During this process, he received protests and negative feedback by the authorities over what they deemed to be a negative connotation with the name "Virgin." They thought it had nothing to do with what his services were at the time, which focused on music before the company became a worldwide conglomerate and philanthropy organization. However, Branson believed that Virgin was the ideal name because it was all about something new, something fresh, first time, denoting a willingness to explore. After sharing that perspective, the authorities then granted him the appropriate intellectual properties and the ability to build that brand as he has done so well.

Branding is your logo, but it's far more than that. It is your website, but it's more than that. It's where you live. It's what kind of car you drive. It's what you wear when you're not at work and what you wear when you are at work. It's where you went to school. It's where your kids go to school. It's what church you go to. It's what church you choose not to go to. Pretty much anything and everything can help you shape and build your personal brand.

When people look at someone like Richard Branson—arguably one of the most valuable brands on the market today—they think of him not just as a billionaire entrepreneur, they also think of him as an adventurer, a thrill seeker, a wise business person, a charitable person and a philanthropist. There are so many things that go into his personal brand because he's done such an amazing job of building it.

Your job, as a small-business owner, is to brand yourself as well as Richard Branson did with a much smaller budget.

How you do that? You start with the basic tools and you recognize that branding is a mentality and is something that you should be doing nonstop. There is virtually no time where you shouldn't be branding. For example (Topher speaking), John Spencer Ellis has done an amazing job of branding himself as the ultimate go-to guy for fitness marketing and running a successful business in the fitness industry; that is just one of the ways that he has branded himself exceptionally well.

The basic branding tools

The most basic concept is your logo. Why are logos important? Logos are critical because every human being responds to a part of their brain known as the reptilian brain, which has everything to do with recognizing and responding to symbolism and pictures.

Your logo will consist of three main components:

1. The first component is your **company name**.
2. The second component is your **slogan**.
3. The third component is your **icon.**

Coming up with a company name

First off, let's start with your company name because it's probably the most controversial piece of the puzzle. When naming your company, the goal is to use the name that is most commonly associated with what it is that you do already for your current customers. So in other words, if you could open up your customers' brains and go to the file folder tab that has your company name on it, what would that name be? Would it be Widgets Incorporated, or would it be Jennifer Smith, your actual name?

If you're in the service industry and you're focused on building relationships with your customers, the most important name that they will remember is your personal name, not some fancy company or corporate name. While not everyone should name their company after themselves, if you're trying to develop a personal brand, it's the fastest and the easiest way to do it.

Some of the objections from entrepreneurs regarding this notion are that they fear that something will go wrong in the company, such as a public case of poor customer service, which will then forever be associated with them personally. We think that provides pretty great motivation to ensure that you always have the best customer service.

We both have John Spencer Ellis and Topher Morrison, our names and likenesses, incorporated into our work. Because of that, we are very careful about how we treat customers. If someone gets upset about something, how do we handle that? Do we give them refunds willingly and easily if they want it?

All of those things are about making sure that we protect our brand identities. If you Google either of our names, you will discover that Google's a pretty good friend of ours. We have both focused long and hard on doing a very good job maintaining a good brand identity.

Using your own name also allows—especially in today's collaboration economy with the immediacy of information and the way personal relationships are built both online and off—people to get to know who you are by what you allow to be seen and known, and that allows for the development of better and stronger relationships.

If they feel like they know you, it's easier to trust you.

If they know you and trust you, they will also probably like you. **Know, like and trust are the three things that are necessary to build quality relationships, improve sales and grow your business.**

On the other hand, there are times when using your personal name is inappropriate and unwarranted. When John Spencer Ellis created his fitness association NESTA (National Exercise and Sports Trainers Association), which provides fitness education for professionals all over the world, he recognized that people would want to earn a fitness certification from an entity larger than just one person. Even though he leads this organization and has a team of world-renowned experts who help manage it on a daily basis, people did not necessarily want to earn a professional certification from John Spencer Ellis or John Spencer Ellis and Team. They want the validity that a NESTA certification will give them and the perspective that they belong to something great.

When he recently acquired and established a U.S. online university and went through a rebranding process with it, John eventually chose the name of Wexford University. First of all, because it is a new brand and it's a university, John recognized that people would want to earn a degree from an established entity, since it would give them more credence, more credibility, more social proof. If an institution seems too nouveau or too fresh out-of-the-box, it may not provide the necessary prestige that your potential students want.

John and his wife Kelli both have Irish ancestry, and so they looked for a place that seemed old world in the UK with a cool name that sounded established like "Oxford," but was certainly unique. The duo even used Wikipedia to search names of cities throughout the UK; when they came upon Wexford and liked the name and the way it sounded, they did a little historical research on the city of Wexford, which is found in the southern part of Ireland and is a popular vacation destination. It has some beautiful castles and is also where the Kennedy family originated. Even better, the nearly impossible to acquire .edu domain was available, sealing the deal with the name of Wexford University.

Again, this became an entity far greater than just one individual and something that gave the feeling of being established, but it's also portrayed and perceived as cutting edge through technology and communications with students and faculty. This process and name allowed for the immediate interpretation of something that had great value and credibility.

With that said, sometimes you will want to use your name for your business and sometimes you will want to research and come up with other options.

Think for a few moments about your unique situation: Who are you trying to appeal to? What product or service do you offer? And does it require more of an institutional type of approach to have the established credibility that's necessary?

One of the other objections that we often hear is, "Well, if I name my company after me, nobody will know what I do." First off, it's not the objective of a company name to ever identify what it is that you do anyway. Google doesn't say what it does by the company name, and even Facebook isn't really related to what the company does.

Company names are just company names. The way people identify what it is that you do is through your slogan, so don't worry about your name not reflecting what your business does, it shouldn't. Your name should reflect who you are and your slogan should represent what you do.

Another objection we hear as to why people can't name their company after their name is they think that they won't be able to sell it should the company grow to a level worthy of a buyout. This is a false notion. If you have a great company that bears your personal name, that doesn't mean you can't sell it with that name. You absolutely can. If you could buy Richard Branson Coaching Programs or Richard Branson Financial Planning or Richard Branson Lifestyles—anything with his name on it—if you could somehow persuade him to let you buy his name, I'll bet you that you would snap it up in a heartbeat. The same thing likely goes for Walt Disney Coaching Programs, Walt Disney Auto Mechanic or Walt Disney anything—the name itself is pure magic.

Your company name should be easy to remember. However, the reality is that most people don't really care about the name of your company, unless it's somehow offensive. When entrepreneurs are interested in purchasing a business, what they're essentially buying is the market share; they're not buying the name. And all companies that are bought by another company end up usually going through what they call a "merge and purge" process. So, for example, when AOL bought out Time Warner, it became AOL Time Warner. Shearson Lehman Brothers used to be two different companies and then they merged and it became Shearson Lehman.

Take a look at the Shearson name over time:

Shearson Hammill & Co., 1901–1974, an investment banking and brokerage firm founded by Edward Shearson
Shearson Hayden Stone, 1974–1979, formed through the merger of Shearson, Hamill and Hayden, Stone & Co.

Shearson Loeb Rhoades, 1979–1981, formed through the merger of Shearson Hayden Stone and Loeb Rhoades & Co.

Shearson/American Express, 1981–1984, formed through the acquisition of Shearson Loeb Rhoades by American Express

Shearson Lehman/American Express, 1984–1988, formed through the acquisition of Lehman Brothers Kuhn Loeb

Shearson Lehman Hutton, 1988–1990, formed through the acquisition of E.F. Hutton & Co.

Shearson Lehman Brothers, 1990–1993

This is just one example among many of how corporations have merged or changed company names in times or mergers or company purchases. There are loads of examples how corporations have merged the two company names.

People have no problem buying a name as long as it's got a good reputation, and what defines reputation typically is the market share. So if you build your business up to a level where you own a significant level of market share, your prospective customers won't care what the name is; they will, however, care what the market share is and that's what they will purchase. Whether or not they keep your name is irrelevant. You can keep that. You can sell it.

In the case of Wexford University, John acquired the approval and recognition by government authorities as well as the opportunity to continue the university and then stripped it bare and built it from scratch. By purchasing this existing opportunity and allowing for some grandfathering, this simple step saved hundreds of thousands, if not millions, of dollars and not months but years of time, which also has an inherent value that was far more appealing than an ugly name and the lackluster logo that was previously in existence.

Coming up with the perfect slogan

Once you have established your company name, you can move on to determining its slogan. Essentially, a slogan should be somewhere between three to seven words (absolutely no more than nine, because you want it to be memorable).

Your company slogan should say one of two things:

1. What you do and the benefit that you provide
OR
2. What you do and who you do it for

And if you just keep it that simple, you'll come up with a great slogan. A terrible slogan is one that has absolutely no tangible identification as to what it is that your business does. For example, "feel the magic, "committed to excellence" or "empowerment beyond measure." While you hear this type of slogan all the time, they are absolutely worthless. Even if they were believable, and many of them aren't, they do not create a clear picture inside the person's head and they don't identify who your target audience is.

When brainstorming ideas for your company slogan, ask yourself "What do I do?" and "Who do I do it for?" Your answers might be simply: I sell widgets. And to homeowners. A great slogan would be "Widgets for homeowners." Or: I'm a life coach. For women over age 40. Then you have: Life coaching for women over 40. Your slogan can truly be that simple.

In many cases, small businesses slogans need to be dumbed down a little, a little less creative, so that they can answer those two important questions. If you can be creative while answering those at the same time, fantastic. When possible, keep it simple. Remember to ask yourself, "What do I do?" and "Who do I do it for?"

Our mutual friend, Ryan Lee's slogan is simply: "Success Simplified." It's two words and it is also alliterative with the two "s" sounds, making it easy to roll off the tongue and easy to remember. It's simple success; it's success simplified. Ryan is a business coach who puts together a variety of life events, and this simple, strong and succinct slogan has worked really well for him.

John Spencer Ellis' slogan? Fitness and Personal Development Solutions. Working with fitness and personal development professionals and providing solutions, this is the slogan that really makes sense. It's that simple.

If you can't identify what you do, and whom do you do it for; ask yourself, what do you do and what benefit it provides. What is John's benefit? He provides solutions and whom does he do it for? Fitness professionals and professional development professionals. Ryan Lee, what is his solution? He makes things simple. What does he make: Success—Success Simplified.

If you keep it that clean and that simple, then you will have a great slogan. If you try getting too creative and too colorful, you likely end up with a meaningless slogan that might look good on your business card and make you feel warm and fuzzy, but does absolutely nothing to drive your business.

Business icons

The next element of branding is your business icon:

The icon is a symbolic representation of what you stand for.

It is not a symbolic representation of what you sell.

Too many small business owners and marketers think that their icon needs to be a symbol of the product or service that they represent, yet this is simply not true. If that were true, Nike's symbol would be a shoe. If that were true, Virgin Atlantic's icon would be a plane or a record or whatever their other 300 companies sell.

The icon is a symbolic representation of what you stand for, and, in many respects, it is for your own personal compass more than for your clients' benefit or good.

The best icons are trained; the public does not immediately recognize them. If you take a close look at the most valuable icons on the planet, such as the Nike swoosh, the Coca-Cola wave and McDonald's golden arches, those icon are popular because they've been around forever, and they are on everything these companies produce. These icons have become synonymous with the company name. Your icon needs to be everywhere your company name is— no ifs, ands or buts.

In creating your logo or icon, you are creating design, and this should also be simple. Think of the Eiffel Tower. Now think of the Golden Gate Bridge. Strip away everything except two identifying lines or curves in each of those iconic landmarks. With the Eiffel Tower, for instance, if you were to make two sweeping strokes with a pencil on paper, could you identify it as the Eiffel Tower? Likewise, what two lines or shapes would you have for the Golden Gate Bridge? It's pretty simple, isn't it?

The same goes for the Nike swoosh and the Coca-Cola wave and other strong, emblematic icons and logos. This is what you need to have in mind whenever possible: Because everyone is so inundated with information and because people often go on information purges, you need something that is quickly identifiable, easily absorbed and easily recalled with as little stimulus as possible. Simple and memorable.

Tag your business with the perfect tagline

Once you have developed a company brand, then you need to look into developing your product brands, because it's very common for a company, even a small one, to have more than one product. Together, all of those product names will work to build and add value to your corporate brand or your personal brand identity. When it comes to your company's tagline, you have a variety of options to consider.

One popular practice is known as alliteration. In using alliteration, your tagline would have two words or more in your name, tagline or product name that start with the same sound.

Interestingly, the human brain likes repeating sounds. Think about Coca-Cola, Kit Kat, Tic Tac and other businesses that use alliteration to great effect.

In addition, rhyming can be a great tagline convention. If you've ever written poetry or songs or paid attention to their wording, a rhyme (and it doesn't have to be a perfect one) can be really catchy and memorable. Certainly, you don't want to be too cutesy when it comes to alliteration or rhymes, but both of these can work well in small business taglines.

Again, it's important to remember that you're ultimately creating a product versus a company name. You have the John Spencer Ellis brand and then within that, you have the product brand, such as Kung Fu Fitness, Fitness Fortunes or Tactix, all of which are memorable product names and alliterations.

Another great example of this is a company brand such as Ford, which then encompasses a product brand like Mustang. It is definitely okay to be more creative with product names.

Much of this information is garnered from arguably the best personal branding guru in America, Peter Montoya. He has two books, which are exceptional for anybody in the service business to read: "*The Brand Called You*" and "*The Personal Branding Phenomenon*". We highly recommend both books if you're looking for additional information on branding.

Do I need to hire someone to help me with all of these branding elements?

The short answer: Probably.

Unless you have solid experience in crafting logos and creating top-notch marketing materials for businesses, you will likely need to hire an expert—you can find a reliable and skilled contractor through a company such as 99 Designs or Elance.com. If you think you're going to have long-term needs for branding support, you might consider hiring someone part time or even full time, depending on your business and your particular needs.

The same goes for all the written elements that go into your business and branding: Make sure you find a good writer to handle your website, marketing materials, press releases and more.

While none of these materials need to be flashy or fancy, they do need to be polished and professional, since they are often the first thing people see when they're looking for someone in your line of business. If your website doesn't draw attention and if your logo is not compelling, then you risk losing potential customers and fans.

Granted, these are extra investments into your business, but they will be well worth it. You will save time and energy by finding a branding professional that can help support all of your business branding efforts.

FRIENDS ARE
MORE RELIABLE
THAN THE INTERNET

I n case you don't already realize it, your friends are much more reliable, especially when talking about the collaboration economy, than the Internet. This chapter is all about tapping into that friendship and reliability. Once you have established your brand identity, the next step is to take that brand and spread it to the masses.

Obviously, social networking is here to stay, and it's going to be a fundamental part of how you market your business and live your life in general. The interesting thing is that when social networking took off, it created a bit of a psychological monster, and now we're starting to see somewhat of a swing in the opposite direction.

In the beginning, for example, with Facebook, it was all about how many friends you could collect. With MySpace (remember that?), everyone wanted to hit more than 5,000 or 10,000 friends. Again, it was all about seeing how many friends you could collect. We automatically approved every friend request. Yet, that's not always the case these days.

Frankly, it only makes sense to connect with people who are genuinely friends or those who have things of value or interest to you within their online profiles. It's okay to say no, and it's ok to ignore the numbers—quality is definitely more important than quantity. In many respects, collecting as many friends on possible Facebook, Twitter, LinkedIn, Sunzu, Instagram, Pinterest and all of the other popular sites is kind of like being a modern-day stamp collector. Instead of collecting stamps, it's all about collecting virtual friends.

Personal pages and business pages

Rather than fan pages and groups, a better way of looking at online social networking is your personal page and your business page. A personal profile is where you are likely to share more personal stories and photos. A business page is just the opposite; this is where you will share the latest information regarding your business.

If you ask 100 social media gurus, you will probably receive 100 different responses to this question: "How much personal and how much business information do I put on my personal page and my fan page, which is my business page?"

We recommend an 80/20 ratio—the same rule that we apply to so many other things in business. In general, your personal page would be 80% personal and about 20% business, and your business or fan page can be 80% business and 20% personal.

If you choose to use online groups, this percentage will vary depending if it's an open group or a closed group. There are many different variables and parameters you can use for creating a group on Google, and those groups are very, very specific in nature with a specific intent and a specific profile of the group members; in these cases, the group members generally get upset if there is too much self-promotion or too much deviation from the main topic of the group.

Further, to maintain your personal and professional sanity, it is necessary to put things in their proper place, and to be able to organize your life with some rules and parameters. Sometimes you need some space and a buffer around these different types of relationships.

Types of relationships in a collaboration economy

We have our family, which can be defined either through marriage or blood. Then you have your friendships, which can be at a distance or up close; these relationships can be deep relationships or casual ones. It is the difference between knowing someone's life story and making a casual acquaintance in passing at an industry conference.

By making the distinction between close friends and acquaintances, you are simply organizing and prioritizing based on the quality and the depth of the relationships in your life. As you continue to grow your brand and your business, the amount of information you will receive will double, then triple, then skyrocket, and you will also have more people who want to be your friend and who want to tell the world that they are your friend. These people may very well place undue, unwarranted and unwelcome demands on your time, which can inhibit your happiness, your sanity and your productivity—both in your business and your personal life. So use some constraint and categorize these relationships, then you can use social media to bolster the best relationships.

Be careful with "brand cuddling," where you use someone else's name to build business or credibility or allowing someone else to do the same to you. If someone uses your name as a reference and a resource, make sure you truly believe in what they have to offer.

Remember, it takes about three steps more to unfriend someone on Facebook than it does to accept a friendship, so choose your friends wisely. Likewise, you must be willing to make a change sometimes.

Always choose quality over quantity

In the new economy, one of the most powerful things that small business owners need to realize is that it's never about the quantity of your database, rather it's about the quality of your database, and who's actively listening to you and interacting with you.

For example, we grow a little concerned about Twitter profiles that are following far more people than those that are following them, because they're really not listening to that many people. In our case, we don't simply follow other people just because they follow us. In the cases where we genuinely care what someone else has to say and offer, then, of course, we do. Likewise, it's flattering to have someone following you, but make your choices based on business sense.

If you're wondering how effective your social media platform is, send out one line via Twitter or Facebook that includes some sort of call to action. Maybe it's a link to a blog or maybe it's of a free download that you have just created for your list. Regardless of the call to action, track how many people take advantage of it. If you have 10,000 followers on Twitter and only 50 people download something free, you don't have a very strong listening audience there. It's not about size or numbers in the new economy; it's about a focus on efficient and smaller levels of high quality.

One of the best examples is centered on one of the newest social networking sites called Unation.com. Unation is a social network platform designed to have you only associate with people who are within business interests or personal interests, rather than mass quantities of people. This site does a very good job of clarifying the difference between the two, so you don't end up sending your relatives free downloads and you don't end up sending your clients the picture of your new puppy.

When developing and honing your lists, be highly picky, be selective, and don't accept anyone and everyone. Focus on the people, your target audiences, who show some level of interest in your particular business. You will have less to manage AND your business will reap the rewards. This is a good lesson in general for the collaboration economy.

BECOMING A KEY PERSON OF INFLUENCE IN THE INDUSTRY

Becoming a key person of influence or KPI in your industry is a key factor in your business' success.

Topher has a great story about becoming a key person of influence within your industry…

"I've been in the personal development business for almost 25 years and I've seen this industry go through some amazing transformations. By the word amazing, I don't mean in a good way. This industry has been overrun with so many people putting out such mediocre to poor content, which is generally nothing more than a copy of a copy of a copy of somebody else's information. All of this got me to the place where I was ready to get out of the entire speaking business simply because I didn't want to associate myself with the personal development market any longer."

About three years ago, one of my promoters in London wrote a book. The book, which we've referenced, was called 'How to Become a Key Person of Influence' by Daniel Priestly. As that book was coming out, I was getting ready to get out of the industry. Nevertheless, I slowly watched his book rise through the charts to become a bestseller, and then I watched him develop it into a growth accelerator program, where he started working with no more than 50 businesses at a time for a 40-week program. I started to see the results he was producing for entrepreneurs who had great ideas great products, but who didn't know how to market themselves or their business in this new economy.

What I saw was nothing more than an entrepreneurial revolution to the point where, when he systematized his program, he contacted me and offered me the U.S. sector of his business, and I turned it down because I was tired of personal development. Yet, I kept watching his success and kept contemplating what I would be doing with my life, and I finally realized that what he was offering wasn't a personal development program. It was business development, and I believe that what personal development was to the 1970s, business development is going to become for this new generation. It made me have a change of heart."

Since that change, I've gone on to collaborate with Daniel on the 2nd edition of the book written specifically for the American market.

If you are interested in learning more, you can download the first two chapters of "How to Become a Key Person of Influence" for free at www.keypersonofinfluence.com/usa. Much of the information we share here will be culled from this book as well.

We have realized that people with issues in life tend to have a variety of limiting beliefs and fears. Likewise, we have now discovered that successful entrepreneurs like Bill Gates, Steve Jobs and the rest also have these limiting beliefs and fears. These realizations make personal development redundant, because the reality is that successful people and unsuccessful people both have emotional issues. Emotional issues, limiting beliefs and fears, however, do not determine whether someone succeeds or doesn't succeed. The ultimate determining factor in success is whether the small businessperson has put specific strategies into place to support their business.

For starters, take a look at how people get into business today. There are three types of entrepreneurs:

1. **The first level or outer ring is for newbies:** This is where newbies make their entrance into running a business. They are the people who are so thrilled to be in any business that they don't even care if they make any money. They are just happy to be there. They can work 20-hour days and the time flies by. They're all about getting out and meeting as many people as they can. They tell everybody what they do. They shout it from the rooftops and they're just excited to be in the business, whether it's real estate or a pet shop or financial planning or dentistry or massage therapy or personal training. It doesn't matter. They are just thrilled to be there. This phase tends to last from 9-12 months before this group of business owners jumps to the next level.

2. **The second level or middle ring is a worker bee:** This level is where the majority of all entrepreneurs and business owners stay for life. Worker bees probably work similar hours to the newbies, but they no longer enjoy it. They are a little bit embittered. They even look at the newbies with a bit of envy like, "Oh, I remember the day when I had that level of naivety and innocence," and they wish they could get that back, but they can't because now they're wise to the market. They've discovered and realized how hard it is and how competitive it is. They got into the business thinking they had the most original, unique concept or idea but about a year later, they realized that there are at least another 20 people in their exact neighborhood that have the same concept or product or service, and so they have to work really hard to compete for a limited amount in the market. They are on the phone all the time; they're chasing down the leads and they see the newbies. The worker bees see another group of individuals as well. The individuals that they notice are the key people of influence.

3. **The third level or inner ring is the key person of influence:** These are the business owners who don't seem to have to chase the business down. Their phone rings. People contact them. It's not uncommon for the worker bees to look at the key people of influence with a lot of judgment. They sit there and they think, "Why are they getting all the business? I have a far better product. I give far better service, but people keep going to that person. Why are they choosing them instead of me?" They wish they could become that key person of

influence, but they don't know how to do it. Anyone can become a key person of influence through a very effective five-step process that is perfect for the new economy. You can also learn more about all of this in *"How to Become a Key Person of Influence"* by Daniel Priestley and Topher Morrison.

How to become a key person of influence in 5 simple steps

To reach that third level, to become a true key person of influence, you can follow these five steps:

1. **Create a perfect pitch.** Every person of influence in history has been known for his or her perfect pitch, whether it was John Lennon's beautiful "Imagine," whether it was John F. Kennedy saying, "Ask not what your country can do for you; ask what you can do for your country," or Martin Luther King talking about his dream. Mother Teresa is recognized for serving the poor, Martha Stewart is well known for her cakes and crafts, and Richard Branson is known as the rebel billionaire. All of these people are recognized for something. That's what we call a perfect pitch.

    Most business owners, however, can't perfect their pitch because they don't even know whom they're selling their pitch to. If you believe that your market is anybody in the world because everybody would benefit from your product or service, it's time to wise up.

    In the new economy—the collaboration economy— it's all about getting rid of your net, getting your hook, finding that one specific target market and going after it, full steam ahead.

Here is the crux of the collaboration economy: If you are trying to go after everybody, then everybody who you want to collaborate with could essentially be your competition. But once you become a Key Person of Influence, you have a specific target. Then you will discover one of the greatest secrets of key people of influence: KPIs refer business to other KPIs all the time. One of Topher's business partners is Kevin Harrington, the king of the infomercial industry and celebrity investor on the hit TV series "*Shark Tank*" seasons 1–3. In the infomercial industry, Kevin's main "competition" is Greg Renkor. Kevin reached out to Greg one day and expressed that his niche is hard products like fitness equipment or appliances, whereas Greg's niche is soft products like lotions/creams. Kevin's idea was to send Greg all his potential soft product business in the understanding that Greg would send him the potential hard products. The result was they both were able to streamline their product development and generate much more business. KPIs send business to other KPIs.

The key to the collaboration economy is to become a KPI so you can refer business that isn't within your market to other KPIs who will, in turn, send business to you that's outside of their immediate market.

How do you do it? You develop a perfect pitch. Perfect pitch is all about knowing exactly who your customer is, what you can solve for that person and giving yourself the credibility necessary to do it. Once you've established a perfect pitch, then people will know exactly what you stand for, they'll know exactly who your market is and you'll be able to more accurately find those people within your industry.

2. **Now take that pitch and get it published.** The key people of influence in any industry are the ones who are constantly being quoted, constantly being interviewed, constantly being asked what their opinion is on a hot topic. It is absolutely imperative that, as a key person of influence, you get your knowledge, your information and your work published in trade journals, news magazines, newspapers, blogs and, the brass ring of publishing, getting a book. People who have written books are seen as experts; we aren't just referring to a self-published eBook, but an actual printed book. This tip will likely become obsolete in the near future, but currently, there is still a tremendous level of value associated with a printed book.

The biggest question that usually comes along with getting published is: What information should I get out there?

Within the old model of business, the logic was "If you want my knowledge, you have to pay me, and then I'm going to give it to you." The new school of business instead says that, "Here is all of my knowledge; have it for free, and then when you're ready to pay for the experience come see me."

We previously discussed the example of well-known chef Jamie Oliver: You could pay $30 to get a cookbook that has every one of his recipes and you would have access to a great deal of his knowledge in one book, or you could choose to spent $130 for one meal cooked by Jamie Oliver or a Jamie Oliver certified chef at a restaurant.

Today, people are willing to pay for experience over knowledge. Knowledge has become a commodity thanks to the Internet. Remember, people want to see seven hours of free before they are going to pay for your product or service.

If you are wondering what you should get published, you should take the best information you've got and get that into books, get it into trade journals, get it into magazines. Don't be shy. Don't be worried about giving away trade secrets or your best stuff. People will still ultimately come to see you for your experience.

Case in point: Andrew Love and Stephen McIndoe in the United Kingdom, wrote a book called "*Developing and Sustaining Excellent Packaging Labeling and Artwork Capabilities: Delivering Patient Safety, Increased return and Enhancing Reputation.*" (If you think the title is a mouthful, you should read the book!) It's about how to create the perfect label for a prescription medication. Apparently, one of the biggest expenses for the pharmaceutical companies is improperly labeled medication. To that end, this consulting firm, whose specific target niche is pharmaceutical companies that produce mass quantities of medicine, wrote the most detailed, comprehensive, and what many would say, boring book on how to properly label your medication. The company willingly admits that nobody has probably ever read the entire book because it is so detailed that most people tend to give up one or two chapters in and simply decide to call the authors and ask them to do it for them.

As a result, their business has absolutely exploded. Even though the company gave away all of their information in the most comprehensive book possible on this topic, all of a sudden they are now viewed as the experts in their industry, and people look at all the work that they do and say, "I'd much rather pay them to do it for me."

Get your best information out there. Don't be afraid to contact publishers, to use Create Space (self-publishing system) through Amazon.com and to get that expertise in writing in your first book.

3. **Next, productize your intellectual property.** This is simply a big statement that means you need to develop products to support your business and your brand. The first product that you could focus on, for example, would be a book, but beyond that, you can create many more products of interest. In essence, there are two types of products: One is "products for prospects," the other is "products for profit." To get your business up and running, the first product you should create is a product that you sell for prospects, meaning you willingly and easily give it away or sell it for a very low cost simply to track and trap that information. We have done several products together which are what were considered product for prospects. We give away the product but in exchange, we now have a name and e-mail address, a location and we can market to that person. That's the best way to build your list of prospective customers. Once you have enough prospects,

then you can create your second product, which would be a sellable product that you can make for profit.

4. **Raise your profile.** First, make sure that you are very easy to find on Google. When people type in your name, your business should be found on the first page on Google's search results.

Even if you have a beautiful website and amazing content, if your website is not organized, structured and created in a way which is pleasing to Google's ever changing algorithms, many people will never see your site and you will make far fewer sales. That is a simple fact.

You can drive more traffic to your site through several means, including paid advertising. The top returns that you typically see on a Search Engine Results Page (also called "SERP") are paid for—these businesses are willing to invest some money to pay to make sure they are at the top of the search engine results page. Naturally, this can get very expensive, and it requires ongoing strategy, skill and monitoring as well as an understanding of the analytics and a specific budget. Many of these will be scarce when you're starting a small business. Further, even when they are well established, many entrepreneurs still choose not to do this. It definitely has a cost. It definitely has a benefit. If you are going to pursue this option, take the time to do some additional research.

Another option is to focus on coming up in the natural search or the "organic search," which simply means that your website is written and organized to appeal to Google, and that it is highly specific and relevant to the people who search Google to find what it is that you offer.

Google regularly updates its algorithm. Two of its most famous updates have been called "Penguin" and "Panda," each with their own attributes, yet each disdain spamming, overstuffing of keywords and meaningless links to and from other websites.

Each time an algorithmic change takes place, small businesses can either prosper or perish, so you need to make sure that your website is always in Google's good graces. You can do that by not being solely reliant on one methodology for attracting people to your website.

Besides being easy to find on Google, you also need the traffic that comes from social media. You also need to have traffic that comes in from press releases. You need to have traffic that comes from other industry-related blogs, which is very, very important and is generally highly underused and highly underrated. Your business will shine in both the eyes of the consumer and the Google gods if you have great online peer reviews, which indicate that you are a Key Person of Influence within that industry and that niche. And of course, it's good to get inbound links from a lot of different sites and a lot of different resources. However, Google places far more emphasis and value, and will give you more what is known as "juice," if you have inbound links from other KPIs who do something similar to what you do; these will definitely increase your rankings in search results.

John has a great story on just this topic:

This story is a good example of a collaboration economy in action. My wife Kelli, is a very well-respected celebrity interior designer who has been on just about every major network including HGTV, TLC, NBC and Bravo. Recently, she decided that she wanted to help other interior designers grow their businesses as well.

So with our combined creative and entrepreneurial spirits and interests, the two of us collaborated on this idea. I was excited to assist Kelli and her business partner, Lori Dennis, who is also a celebrity interior designer, create their business, which they named Design Camp. Even though they both are industry icons and have had tremendous success (in fact, they are both ranked in the top two percent of their industry), more than three quarters of all referrals coming to their website and signups for their $1,200 program are hailing from an industry-related blog. If these industry-related blogs did not exist, or they did not tout them as a Key Person of Influence, this would be another story entirely. Three quarters of their revenue for the year would be gone, just like that. So even though Kelli's SEO or Search Engine Optimization is good, being a KPI and being mentioned on other industry blogs is now contributing to three quarters of her annual income, which we both think is truly amazing.

In addition, both Kelli and Lori have books, and they are currently working on another book together, which will bring in different people who have gone through their interior design camp. This industry has a true sense of community and collaboration with these key persons of influence far and above what I could have ever expected and imagined, and these industry bloggers are so prominent, prevalent and influential that they have become the star speakers at the Design Camp events. The attendees are just as interested in meeting with them, learning how they do what they do and taking celebrity photos with these bloggers who have become, by default and through their own means, KPIs.

Blogs, as you likely know, can also lead to books. If you are still wondering, 'How will I write a book?' the best way is to start writing a blog and that will organize your thoughts, get you structured in terms of what your message should be, and then you can take all of the information from the blog and get it published—restructure it, have it edited, and you can have yourself a book within a year easily.

Kelli did one more great thing in terms of being a KPI and getting published. She combined her blog posts, various articles from local publications and her expertise, and turned that into an educational program through our coaching school, the Spencer Institute, where people can now become a Certified Design Psychology Coach. It's a hybrid of interior design, environmental psychology, color therapy and life coaching. Then she took that a step further and made that into her book titled *"Do I Look Skinny in This House?"* It all works together to add up to impressive success as a key person of influence in the design industry.

In addition, it's important to recognize that traditional media still has a very important place and a very important role. Not only do you want to raise your profile online, but you want to raise your profile on TV and on radio and Internet radio and Internet TV – everywhere!

Branding never doesn't work. That is intentionally a double negative. The reason is because if you have that opportunity to get on TV; whether it is a local morning show or a major national news show, if you haven't been trained on how to get on that camera and speak in the appropriate way, you will never get asked back. You can do far more damage to your brand than if you had never been on TV at all. To that end, it's important to get the proper level of training up front before the opportunity happens. Opportunities to get on TV are very quick. You're never going to have a TV studio call you up and say, "We're going to do a piece on the proper type of solar panels to install on your home in about a month or so. Would you please get prepared so we can interview you?" You are most often told, "We're doing a spot tonight. Can we interview you within the next three hours?" Time is always of the essence when it comes to the media, so being prepared is key.

If you've ever been on TV, and you thought you did a decent job of it, here's a great litmus test for you: Did that TV show call you back to have you on a second time? If the answer to that question is no, then you need to get media trained pronto. If you have been trained on speaking and interacting with the media, you will always get asked back because you'll do what they want you to do without them having to tell you. They'll never tell you. They will just let you look like a fool on TV without correcting it and then move on to someone and something else. If you look at some of the most successful entrepreneurs who have their own TV shows today, it's because they were great guests when they were on somebody else's show. Rachael Ray, Dr. Phil and Dr. Oz all rose to fame after being guests on Oprah Winfrey's long-running talk show. They became so well known and beloved as guests that the networks eventually offered them their own shows (with a little help from Oprah).

5 quick media tips:

- Write down three key points before the interview and practice weaving them into conversation.
- Keep answers short and clear, positive and friendly.

- Avoid industry jargon—keep it simple.
- Avoid discussing customer relationships, acquisition rumors or competitors (unless you have something nice to say).
- Be responsive. Get back to reporters within the hour. If you don't have an answer to their question, promise to follow up and make sure you do so.

Even if you're savvy business owner who's quite comfortable up on stage and speaking to groups of people, the rules for speaking to a live audience are different. Virtual and live audiences are different, so your preparation and delivery has to recognize that. Some of the best live speakers in the world really struggle to develop a presence on camera simply because they're trying to use the same skills that they used to entertain a live audience. It's two different worlds.

A great example of this is Anthony Robbins, who is arguably one of the most powerful and popular professional speakers of all time. If you've never had the pleasure of seeing him speak live, you owe it to yourself at least once in your life to go see the master of professional speaking. He is amazing at in-person, motivational speaking, and yet when he gets on camera and tries to use the exact same skills, he falls somewhat short. This is why everyone wants to see him in person and not on camera. It's simply a different skillset for a different audience.

5. **Develop partnerships with other key people of influence outside of your niche to bring their clients into your niche.** Of course, you will never be able to get through to another KPI if you're not a KPI yourself. You'll

never be able to have other KPIs refer business to you until you have hit the same level of status and influence.

When you start a company in any industry, until you become a key person of influence, your full-time job needs to be becoming a key person of influence. Most people do the exact opposite. They focus on trying to develop the best service, the best product or the best anything, and they don't worry about becoming a key person of influence. Then they get stuck in the rut of being a worker bee and can't figure out why they're not getting the right business and more of it.

If you are in a service industry and you can honestly say that you are not a key person of influence (one way of knowing that you're not a key person of influence is if you haven't taken a vacation in at least one year, and if you work more than 40 hours a week), then you need to focus your full-time efforts on becoming a key person of influence within your industry before you focus anymore on your business.

Altogether, these five tips will take you a long way towards developing influence, contacts, connections and the business of your dreams.

THE FUTURE
OF FINANCE

With all of that down pat, the next step is another big one: How are you going to monetize your business?

If you look at the economic stability or instability of the United States, European countries, Australia and others, all of these areas have experienced or are currently in the midst of financial turmoil. Simply put, there is widespread instability in financial markets across the globe.

The benefit in all of this instability, however, is that the savvy business owners who understand the new collaboration economy will soon discover that the stability of your personal currency is not nearly as important to running a successful small business as it used to be.

If you look at the currencies in the world today, you will quickly discover that there is a new type of currency which is worth more than the dollar, the euro, the pound, the yen or anything else, and that is individual currencies or private currencies.

The power of private currency

What is private currency?

If you were to open up your smart phone and look at how many apps you have for companies which allow you to buy their products or services based upon the points that you earn by being a loyal customer, you already understand private currency. For example, with a quick glance of our Passbook apps on our iPhones, we can determine that we have private currency from Starbucks, Walgreens, the United Airlines Gate Check Pass and more. These are just a few of the companies that offer these types of valuable loyalty rewards. If you fly enough to earn them, you can later fly anywhere in the world for free based upon the currency that every airline uses called frequent flier miles. You can drink a venti dark roast coffee for free based upon the private currency that Starbucks has called Reward Stars. You can get free products at CVS and at Walgreens; you can get free pizzas at your favorite local pizza store. Essentially, you can buy virtually any type of product based upon loyalty points built up through all of these companies, and that is an actual currency.

The more unstable the economy becomes, the more reliable private currency is going to become. Even within this generation, companies may be able succeed without having any U.S. or UK or Australian currencies being used whatsoever. They might be able to thrive solely and wholly on their individual company currencies. And in many respects, we are going back to the former days of bartering, where we have certain products of value.

We will definitely witness a huge increase in the various types of private currencies you can get online where you sign up and register as a client and then you can sell your products for points and you can buy products for other points. With this scenario, you will virtually be able to live your entire life using these membership clubs where you can buy and sell and trade point systems for your products.

While this is still a little ways down the road, the savvy entrepreneur today will start building this type of currency into his or her business model right now. Ask yourself how you can develop loyalty reward programs. How can you sell gift cards to your customers so that they can then come back and just give you your own private credit card? The answers to these questions will take your business far.

While this idea of private currency works great now, that hasn't always been the case...

In our country's earliest days when the Western portion of the country was being settled, mining was one of the primary industries, and travelers, fortune seekers, entrepreneurs and people who, at some times had no other choice, would become an indentured servant of sorts to the mine. It generally worked something like this: A person would come and work in the mine all day and would then get paid with a currency that could only be redeemed at the company store; all of the things that they could buy at the company store would be things that were needed for survival. Certainly, this is a pretty unethical and inappropriate way to do business and manage private currency, but it shows that the general concept is not new.

What you need to do is use this concept in a way that is ethical, appropriate, helpful and based on equality, in such a way that serves and helps people and provides what they need, while helping you grow your business at the same time.

This general concept of bartering or developing your own private currency and creating your own value for what you do, for what you offer, for who you are and for what your company stands for, is nothing new. It's just a matter of redesigning it for the new collaboration economy.

EXPERT INTERVIEWS

Following are interviews with great examples of early adopters; people who understand, participate in and succeeded in the collaboration economy.

Each individual has a different story, different experiences and different perspectives, and they each provide living examples of how a collaboration economy can be hugely successful in a variety of businesses.

We are proud to introduce our team of collaboration experts: Yanik Silver, Debbie Allen, Ryan Lee, Paula Bauer and Kevin Harrington.

INTERVIEW WITH YANIK SILVER

Maverick Entrepreneur, Author and Publisher

John: Yanik is a friend and someone I truly admire. Although he did not know it, he was my first coach in writing and direct response marketing. Because Yanik Silver is a leader in sales and marketing and promotion, when I was first learning, I would read his ads in various trade and consumer publications and I thought they were incredibly compelling. They immediately got me interested in the topic and, of course, the products and services that he offers.

I have three questions for Yanik and the first one is: In today's economy, what are the three best ways for business owners and entrepreneurs to collaborate?

Yanik: I really like this idea of collaboration. I have three words that I've been using recently that describe what we have been doing and what we've been moving towards. It's all about connecting, co-creating and catalyzing, which all impact collaboration and the co-creation of our world.

The biggest collaboration opportunity right now for business owners is to put their end-user on their team to help them "manufacture" or create an ideal product or service to put out there. Technology has enabled us to be really cognizant of what is going on in the marketplace through feedback. A lot of people love surveys, but I have some different feelings on surveys.

I really like people voting with their wallets more so than anything else, because they're not going to lie when it comes to where they're spending their money and making their purchasing decisions. They are only going to buy what they really want.

One of the most unique things to come around in the last couple of years, and continues to gain traction, are things like Kickstarter, Indiegogo and other crowdfunding platforms. To me, the most exciting part about all of these is that you can easily gauge marketplace demand. If you're not familiar with these platforms, you can put out a project—let's say you want to create a new journal that you're going to sell to other people. It's a beautiful, leather-bound journal—but instead of going off to some leather manufacturer in Italy and securing all of this leather and putting it together and then storing 2,000 journals in your basement or garage and hoping you sell them, you put out something on Kickstarter, Indiegogo or one of these other platforms that talks about the exquisite nature of these journals, how they are handmade, what the history is behind them, the type of paper and why you decided to put them together. Then you put out incentives for people to buy the journal. For instance, perhaps if you buy one journal for $25, you get a pre-run with your initials on it. If you buy three journals, you get all three colors of the journal with your initials. If you buy 15 journals for "x" amount, then you get something else, and it goes all the way up and you can create unique experiences, access or special things, creating an interesting offer and helping you build your business.

I have a couple of friends who have done this spectacularly well. The best part about this is you only spend some time putting together a sales video or some copy related to the product, and then people tell you whether they like your idea or not. Both Kickstarter and Indiegogo give you an option of determining a dollar amount. If you decide that you want to raise $25,000, but don't reach that threshold, the funds donated will go back to the person who gave you the money. No equity changes hands at this point. It's almost like a pre-order way to gauge what you're doing. So to me, that's one of the most exciting collaborative methods out there. You can see how that would be really powerful to not have that risk and know if something is going to work or not work.

John: I have heard so many times as of late how crowdsourcing and crowdfunding with places like Kickstarter have launched incredible technology companies and services, which were eventually acquired for millions of dollars.

Yanik: It's really exciting. The other way that I really see businesses collaborating right now—and this is very exciting to me, too—has actually been around for a while. Disney was probably one of the first to really bring this idea into the spotlight and make a lot of money from it. Licensing, a type of collaboration where you have intellectual property or a process or a brand or something, can make sense when you find another company that has distribution or a specific need in mind. In these cases, you can turn 1+1=3 or one 1+1=11 through collaboration.

Licensing really took off in about the 1930s with Disney licensing Mickey Mouse to a handkerchief manufacturer; the manufacturer sold far more handkerchiefs than expected and realized that they had something there. Today, licensing for Disney is a $15 billion enterprise.

You can look at some of the modern companies that have done this in a big way and then extract it back to what it means for many entrepreneurs today. Look at the band KISS. They've licensed more than $1 billion of revenue from everything from KISS coffins for funerals to the typical items such as bedspreads and pillows and action figures. They even have KISS condoms. Donald Trump is also a master at licensing: For the right amount, you can license the Trump name for whatever you want: vodka, water, you name it.

The Angry Birds app is a terrific example of a company that has recently taken off. This team made nearly $50 million in just one year and about one-third of their income comes from licensing, which is significant. They licensed the Angry Bird characters for plush dolls and potato chips.

The best part about licensing is that you get paid—there's almost no cost involved except for the initial sales process or delivering what that other company needs from you.

I've seen licensing work in many different areas, so I will give you a couple of examples just out of my own book where we've collaborated.

One of my very first publishing businesses was selling to cosmetic surgeons and dermatologists interested in acquiring more cosmetic patients. We created a little kit for them that included a little manual and a few other things, which sold for $900 and it was pretty cool. One company told me, "Well, I want to do this in the veterinary business," and I was thrilled. We licensed the materials to him and he paid us 10% or 15% on top of all sales made, so there was leverage and collaboration there where we both brought different strengths to the table. I've done this repeatedly with excellent results.

We have someone in Japan who licenses our materials and sells them and then pays us a percentage back. There are many ways to use licensing and there's a lot of ways you can license. Let's say, for example, that you're really good at processing the waste products from the logs that go through a local lumber mill. That lumber business is a very area-specific kind of business. You're not going to go out and get logs from all across the country because it costs too much for transport. So what they can do is license the process for how make a better ROI out of the waste products and then offer this to other lumber mills across the country that they weren't competing with in their local area, creating a great way of collaborating and essentially taking a hidden asset and turning it into revenue for them.

John: What about being able to identify your strengths and weaknesses and being honest about that, because sometimes as self-directed and motivated entrepreneurs, we are blinded by the illusion that we have the necessary skills to do everything that's possible and needed. How do you do an honest assessment and say to yourself, "I do have this skill; I don't have this skill; I do or do not like to do these things?"

Yanik: On a macro level of a business, there is a very typical kind of SWOT analysis, which is: Strengths, Weaknesses, Opportunities and Threats. This is a good exercise to go through and see where determine those as an organization. On a personal level, one of the things I always think about when I collaborate or when I partner with somebody is that there is no need for two of me. We don't need another Yanik in the mix, so I've spent the past 15–20 years really trying to get to know myself; my true essence and how I can best contribute to any partnership or collaboration.

Part of that is intuitive, part of it comes from journaling, part of it comes from assessment testing, and the other part is really seeing where you get more joy and happiness and where you get meaning out of doing certain tasks. Naturally, nobody likes to do stuff that they don't like to do. In my case, I'm not a super detail-oriented person. My unique abilities, the three things I can do all day and feel more energized at the end of the day than at the start revolve around ideas. Anyone can come to me for an idea for a business, and I can help enhance that idea and make it into a better value-based proposition and something that has unique positioning in the marketplace. I just love that kind of work and thinking. Then the second thing that I'm really great at is creating a platform for connecting with investors. The third thing is instigating a little bit of mayhem and mischief, which is always fun and interesting.

I also love the Kolbe test, which is a really good assessment test that tests your cognitive ability, or the natural way that you strive when you're taking on business tasks. Using this assessment, I learned that I am a "quick start," which means that I will jump into a project without reading the instruction manual or planning far ahead. I love to just jump in on a project or an idea. Other people may tend to be more methodical and really set out a plan when starting a new project or venture. One way is not better than another, but if you know where you fall on the scale and how you operate, then you look for other people who have those collaborative strengths and that's where it gets exciting. It is like putting together some puzzle pieces of people who have the unique abilities and strengths that you lack. Then there is also "Now discover your strength," which is an online assessment that can be really useful when it comes to collaboration and entrepreneurship.

My friend, Chip Connolly, the former CEO of Joie de Vivre, said that the first half of your life is about accumulating and the second half is about editing, so I look at it as whittling away and finding that true part of you that really wants to come out.

Earlier I spoke about creating a platform for other people to collaborate. Let me describe that.

That platform is number three, and it is the big one. This is the one that takes a little bit more effort, but is well worth it and it makes great sense to really work on it.

You want to become the hub as much as possible. On a tactical level, there are always people in our lives who are the top. For instance, if you've got something going on, you're going to call on them and ask, "Hey, do you know somebody who can do this?" or "do you have a great resource for this?" How did they become that hub? For one thing, they are probably just naturally curious people who love to interact with multiple groups of people, companies, platforms and ideas. People who serve as hubs have that role in many areas of their lives. Simply making an introduction without expecting something in return can help you become that hub.

Asking compelling questions is also key. Most people will ask, "What business are you in?" If you're at a business networking event, that's fine, but it's not an exciting or illuminating question. On the other hand, try, "John, what are you most passionate about right now?" or "What are you most excited about?" or "What's the project that you've got the most interest in right now?" These questions reveal so much more. If someone has a business that's doing gangbusters in one place, but their passion is really something else like a new project or a new startup, then that answer will be much more meaningful. If I can make an introduction for that person that can help them along or give them a resource, a book or something that helps them achieve their passion, that's powerful. That's a value add.

On the other side of the equation, there has to be a compelling value proposition on the other person's end, too, if you're going to make introductions that make sense and matter. There is definitely a way of doing introductions that really make sense and help establish you as a hub. Richard Branson, founder and chairman of the Virgin Group, might be in my Rolodex, but I'm only going to facilitate an introduction if it adds value for him as well. Mutual interest and collaboration are key.

The other thing that can really enhance this opportunity for you as that connective point is to start creating events and experiences where you can be the hub. One of my businesses is a local network of entrepreneurs, and part of what I really excel at creating for them is the platform where they can connect in a big way, where deals happen and friendships develop and they grow their business and so forth. You can do that on any sort of scale. It doesn't have to be this epic scale of going to Richard Branson's island for a week or flying in a private jet to a luxury destination. It can be as simple as having a once-a-month dinner and calling it something interesting to encourage networking and introductions. I encouraged a friend who recently moved to create one of these and told her to call it "ACE:" Artists and Creative Entrepreneurs. This creates a reason for people to come together and make in-person connections. Even in this expanded age of global Internet networking, LinkedIn, Facebook, you name it, in-person connections are still incredibly valuable, but it's also about the quality of that in-person connection. In the case of my group, I like to do something unique for dinners that we run. We have what we call "Dangerous Dinners."

John: A couple years back, we were at the same business event and you ordered a double-stretch limo. It drove a group of heavy-hitters around, and we hit up five to eight of Hollywood's hottest restaurants. Then we all got back to the hotel in the wee hours of the morning. It was a blast and memorable. You created an epic evening, which also fostered great business collaborations. You are known for creating an experience for people.

Yanik: These Dangerous Dinners that we have been doing lately have been very interesting; we create a very unique experience such as a theme for the dinner that we keep hidden and mysterious for all of that night's guests. At a recent event, we taught people how to saber off champagne bottles—cut off the tops of champagne bottles to open them with a saber–and then we taught them how to fence. It was called "Swords and Sabers" and all the food was served on sticks and so forth. This type of event doesn't have to be totally over the top, but these types of dinners and events lead to better connections and that experience is definitely something that people are craving. If your event is unique enough, people are going to remember you for bringing them together.

My "Underground" is probably a perfect example of that where we'll have 400-500 people in the audience, and every year we get some of the best real-world doers who are making their money online, who come in and we make it a fun experience like it's a spy team. We also host a variety of special events and parties to make it a lot of fun and unique, so it's different and memorable. When people make partnerships or collaborations or joint ventures there, they remember meeting at the Underground because I was that connective hub—that platform—for them even though I may never have even seen them at that event or even talked to them or personally introduced them. Because of that event, it gives you leverage and that's really powerful.

I also have a friend of mine who puts on events. The main part of the marketing is focusing on events and becoming the hub. They are in the IT world and they invite others from the industry month to their headquarters each month, and then they do something fun and unique for them. It might be learning, it might be a party experience, and the audience generally includes both customers and new prospects. It's just a great way of driving business and being that resource that people look for today.

It also gives you media. For example, at our event, I am able to invite people selectively as my guests and they all look around and will say, "Wow, there are 450 people here and this is an amazing event," and it raises the esteem in their eyes of what our value is to them as well. It's pretty interesting.

John: Yanik, one of the things that I've noticed about you—we've attended several high-level business, entrepreneurial, and marketing events together and you always have a journal with you. Earlier you spoke about journaling and said that it's a way for you to discover a lot about yourself, but it also seems that you are using it to create charts, diagrams and perhaps a little doodling along the way. Even though you and I earn most of our income through electronic means and the Internet, you carry a journal everywhere you go. Why is this?

Yanik: I love the process of writing. The analog technology—there's something to it still that really makes sense and there are scientific studies about journaling that increase as well as interesting books on the value of journaling in an electronic age.

There are a couple of things that I use my journal for most often. One is gratitude where I'll write down everything that I'm thankful for, especially if I'm feeling kind of down and maybe a project is not working the way that I thought it should be or matching up to my ideal vision. Just sitting down and literally writing out all the things you're thankful for puts you in that positive frame of mind. It's really, really powerful and if you continually write in a journal, over time you can flip back and say to yourself, "Oh, that's really great" as you recognize all the good things in your life.

I also use it because when you're writing, it forces you to create a beginning, middle and an end. So, if I'm feeling something going on and trying to sort through some feelings I'm having, writing is really powerful because it stops the jumbled thoughts that are going on in your head. They are always going in and out and cascading around, when writing forces you to have that beginning, middle and end. The effect is really, really powerful.

John: Before we go on to our last question, I wanted to give you a little bit of the neuroscience part of the journaling, and that is when you journal—when you write—two things happen: One is that you write slower than you can type, so you are more conscientious about what you are doing because you have time to unravel the mystery of what it is that you want to write and think about. The second component of that is it is a very distinct kinesthetic or "tactile" action. When you combine learning experiences—visual, auditory, and then, in this case, adding in the kinesthetic/tactile portion—it allows you to be embedded in your subconscious in another way, which creates more neuro-connections in a different part of your brain, which then can cross-reference each other later to have a more complete and fulfilling and exact experience of what you did.

Yanik: I also use it all the time for my maps and diagrams. I'm a big doodler; I love the visual process because it does unlock and open up my brain. Sometimes ideas aren't quite ripe for the harvesting, but I'm a big believer that your ideas can escape you if you don't write them down, so I make notes in my journal whenever I can.

John: I think this is probably the most important question for people who are new to this concept and just getting started. What should a first-time collaborator be cautious of when creating relationships?

Yanik: I think there are many times when collaborating might mean sharing ideas and many people get nervous that somebody is going to steal their idea or that in some way, shape, or form that they are harvesting the scarcity mentality. For me, I don't mind sharing ideas with other people. I think that's the way that we all grow and if you're trying to hide behind your fear of loss, it really hinders the process. I'm all about abundance and realizing that if you get together with other people and you're collaborating with them, typically you're going to end up being in a better position than if you stopped and only tried to do everything on your own. For this to work, you have to be a little more open, a little bit more transparent, a little bit more giving. I also try to avoid keeping a ledger in my head where I add things up like, "Okay, I did this for this person and they didn't do this, so now they owe me this or that." When you focus solely on the quid pro quo, then it becomes transactional. It's a hard way of living your life and creating the relationships that are going to drive you forward. For me, maybe there is a big scoreboard somewhere out there that is a global holistic scoreboard, but I'm not going to keep track of it. It kind of reduces the flow of things coming together.

John: Over the last many years I have been coaching and consulting entrepreneurs, whether they do or do not want to collaborate, whether or not they have an online business, or they have formal education or went to the school of hard knocks, it seems that there is a reluctance based on fear. That is the fear of success and/or failure. What is your best advice to someone who is just paralyzed and hasn't taken those first initial steps but you know when they do, they will skyrocket?

Yanik: Some people can take a giant leap forward and they are okay with that, they can handle the uncertainty that goes with it. On the other hand, some people need to take a little bit more of a stair-step approach, where they slowly build up their confidence and see that stuff is working, they gain momentum and realize success over the course of time.

Right now, we are in this amazing time where you can start a few small side bets and see what happens. As we talked about, Kickstarter is one platform for that—it gives you the chance to put something out there and just see what happens, to see how the marketplace reacts and what feedback you get. I think the hardest part is just getting your idea out there or trying to wait until something is perfect there is never going to be a perfect moment. Even if you just commit to one proactive task a day, which will help to move you forward and then that momentum will continue to build.

John: That's smart advice. Thank you so much. I appreciate you.

Yanik Silver has successfully bootstrapped eight different product and service ideas, hitting the million-dollar sales mark from scratch without funding, taking on debt or even having a real business plan.

He is the author of several best-selling entrepreneurial books and tools. He is the founder of the Underground Online Seminar®, 3% Forward and Maverick1000, a private group of game-changing entrepreneurs which Yanik leads on re-energizing epic experiences.

He is passionate about catalyzing and connecting innovative 21st century entrepreneurs to co-create new business breakthroughs, enhance their happiness and provide greater meaning and impact through their ventures.

www.Maverick1000.com

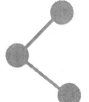

INTERVIEW WITH DEBBIE ALLEN
International Business & Brand Strategist

John: Debbie Allen is my friend and mentor and my first business coach. She is an international business and brand strategist who works with clients to help them gain brand and Internet domination to become a highly paid expert in their industry. She is a best-selling author and one of the world's top professional speakers in marketing mentors. Of course, you can learn more about her at www.debbieallen.com.

Hello, Debbie.

Debbie: Hi, John. It's great to contribute information on collaboration.

John: Thank you so much. First and foremost, I think people need to get the quick version of how we know each other and why I value your opinion so much.

As I told you at the premier of our movie, "*The Compass,*" many years ago, when I was starting my business, I was very motivated,

103

but lacked direction, and I picked up your book, "*Confessions of Shameless Self Promoters*," and it changed my life and it changed my business. I literally had $20 left in my wallet when I went to the then-open Borders Books and bought your book. I read it cover to cover many times through and applied as many strategies as possible, and that was really the turning point in my business. So I first have to thank you for that.

Debbie: You are most welcome. I really did that with exactly what you are talking about—with very collaborative partners, and I was learning along the way as well. Just like you, I found my mentors and interviewed them and put them together, so it's great that this idea keeps going on. This is it! You learn from people and then you share and then you connect with other people and it just keeps connecting. It is a very collaborative way of doing things, so it is my pleasure that I was able to put myself out there, because you never know what can happen when you have the right collaboration partners. That was what happened with that book.

John: I don't think it's crazy of me to say that this book probably wouldn't have been written or even conceptualized if I hadn't read your book, which was a collaborative effort. It's very interesting, isn't it?

Debbie: It's very interesting how that all works. My reason for writing that book, I would like to say it was as brilliant as you in coming together with the idea of collaboration economy. In truth, I really believe that I wrote that book because I wanted to align myself with other people who would actually help my credibility rise and also to put together some really powerful strategies that weren't just coming with me. I think that I had a lot to share but I thought to have a whole book—300 pages of good stuff to share about shameless self-promotion—that seemed like a lot. While there are many great books out there that I respect and that are brilliant, the reason that book was so good is because of that collaborative effort.

The book became very profitable very early on because those people, my collaborators, were all buying books from me. I didn't even expect that to happen and they were all promoting it, so it just got magnified very, very quickly and that's what collaborations like this do. When you are aligned especially with higher-level people, you may be at a higher level yourself. If you want to climb the ladder, you want to align yourself with people either at the same level you are at or higher, and they will kind of start pulling you up that ladder because of their connections and their own collaborations and it just starts magnifying. It's a beautiful thing how it works. One of the best ways to grow your credibility, your expertise, your name in the market is by aligning yourself with other respected people.

John: Yes, and Topher refers to these people as Key Persons of Influence (KPIs) and I often call them the "A Players." Whenever possible, you want to align yourself with A Players or KPIs, and those are the people who you want to collaborate with whenever possible.

Debbie: Right, and they are powerful relationships that you build and that is a skill set that every business person—every entrepreneur—should learn, how to build powerful business relationships. I might not have been the smartest cookie on the block all the time when I was building my businesses, but I did learn that skill. I've been an entrepreneur since I was 19 years old and never went to college, so I learned business from the school of hard knocks and from my relationships—from forming powerful relationships along the way that put these opportunities in front of me. Every time those big opportunities came up, I would kind of shake my head and ask, "Really? Wow, they're noticing that I'm ready for this?"

Sometimes when you have these kinds of partnerships, you are being called out to play a bigger game before you think you are ready. What happens is you feel more comfortable jumping on board because somebody else believes in you and so there are many things that go on behind these opportunities. There's a kind of a mindset when you are aligned with the right kind of people, and the same thing can happen if you're aligned with the wrong kind of people. It is really important to have that connection, and when people believe in you, pay attention and jump up. Right now, there are so many ways to connect—so many more than when I wrote that book because now we're really strong on social media, so it's really easy to build these influential relationships.

I had to build these relationships by writing a great proposal— it was like a book proposal—to get these collaborative people involved in writing for the book, but now you can reach out on social media, get to know people, have conversations going on in chat rooms, you name it. Today there are so many different ways that you can connect, so there's no reason for somebody not to reach out except for fear. Quite often, fear comes from "Well, maybe they think I'm a nobody," or "they don't know me." I remember when I was on the *Howard Stern Show*. He said to me, "Debbie Allen, who are you? I've never heard of you before." I said, "Howard, I'm on your show, aren't I?" I kind of got a one-up with him because I understood already that it doesn't matter if they know you. If they are going to know you, you've got to put your name out there. In the same way, when I put that book together, many people didn't know me, but they respected the ideas that

I had. They respected the collaboration that I was working on. Sometimes you just have a really good idea and people want to jump on board, so it's really important to get the right people on board. When you do reach out to someone, it's really important to "Get your ask in gear," because you've got to be asking. If you think you're not ready, forget it. Get out there and just ask and if it isn't right or you hear the word no, keep on asking.

John: I remember when I was just starting out and I often said to myself and a few other people in my life, "I just need someone to believe in me. I just need the right person to believe in me and be willing to take a risk," and I repeated that again and again. What I didn't realize then, but became apparent over time, is that I didn't bring enough, or the right stuff, to the table to warrant someone's belief in me. What I'm saying is I wanted someone to carry me, perhaps, which now I know is not the right thing to do. What I needed to do was elevate my game. I needed to raise the level that I played at. And, of course, to believe in myself that much more. I needed to do more to make myself more credible and easier to understand. I needed to become more persuasive—I should say "ethically" persuasive because there are certainly other ways to be persuasive. After I learned to raise my game to become a key person of influence and to become an A Player, it was far easier to get other people to believe in me and, therefore have a willingness to collaborate with me. So essentially, you have to prove yourself over time. That's a simple way of putting it.

Debbie: Right. Prove yourself and be a giver, not waiting to always receive the benefit. I've always been that person who wanted to help other people—support other people and before I was successful in many ways, I would always reach out and wonder, "Hey, I just met this person and they do this; who can I refer them to? Whom can I connect them with?" I also do this for my clients; I do this for my business partners; I do this for collaborative partners, daily partners, everybody who I work with. I think, "Hey, they would be a great fit. Where can I refer them?" It's just a habit. It's a constant thing. I don't ask for anything in return, like, "Hey, I threw something your way; throw something my way." I think when you have the right collaborative partners; they say, "Wow! She's done so much. How can I turn around to help her?" I think it comes out when it's ethical persuasion. That's kind of like shameless self-promotion done ethically versus unethically, and if you're always asking for all about me and there's no way of giving back, it's a cycle break.

You have got to be the person who gives and then you receive and you give and receive and give and receive, otherwise you're known in the marketplace as someone who is really pushy or just looking out for themselves. In today's collaborative economy, it is not about being self-centered. It's about supporting other people and when you support other people, you just get raised up and it happens so much faster. People wanting to do more business in this economy should realize that this is really impactful. You don't have to figure it all out by yourself. It's really a supportive thing that moves you up and it's a really powerful source and you know this to be true, John, because you could never have had the amazing progress you've had with "*The Compass*" movie and all the other projects that you have worked on without this collaborative partnership. It would have taken you forever or maybe you wouldn't even be off the ground yet if you were sitting there trying to do it on your own.

John: I believe it would have been impossible, and I'm a person who believes in crazy possibilities. So at the same time, you have to be honest with yourself and say, "I do or do not have these skills, I do or do not have these resources, I do or do not understand the technology, and I do or do not have this connection that's necessary." Ultimately, the reality is that without the collaboration, at least half of what I have done in my life would not have taken place. This is good because this leads me to one of three serious thought-provoking questions I have for you on this topic of a collaboration economy. The first one is this: In the new economy, what is the best way for people to collaborate on business projects?

Debbie: It's really about aligning with the right people. What I do is I teach people to become experts in what they know—highly paid experts in what they know.

You need to know who your competition is and then you need to align yourself with the competition instead of fighting the competition. Now it is very easy to go online and see who else is doing what I'm doing and how can I do it better than them. You can't do it better unless you dominate the Internet with all the things that work around your brand. Once you do, there may be wonderful alliances with people who are doing the same thing you are, which is great. I've always aligned myself with the competition because they are looking for the same target market. So if you have differentiated yourself as a little bit edgier or a little bit differently in some way from that other person, they don't look at you as competition and they will respond, "Hey, let's partner up together. Let's try out some collaborative process in our marketing and advertising and promotions or whatever it is." Because I'm going directly to my target market and I'm just automatically expanding my database with the exact people who I want instead of just hitting it in the dark, it works. It doesn't matter if you have

100,000 people in your database list or your e-mail list if they are not the right target market for your business. You can have just 3,000 people who represent the exact core target market that you want, and that will be far more effective than 100,000 who aren't. I have always aligned myself with all my competitors and sent them business at the same time. As a professional speaker, I was able to send a lot of business to several other speakers. I was also very close to all the people in my niche market. I was very well known in my early speaking years as one of the top retail speakers, so I knew all the other top speakers, too, and they were all friends. We collaborated and shared business back and forth. We even worked on a core project together. I think it's really important to find the people who are already doing what you're doing.

John: How do you identify your strengths and weaknesses so you know who should be your collaborative partner? My guess is that first; you have to be honest about strengths and weaknesses.

Debbie: Right, and many times, you're not and I've gone into the wrong partnership and I've learned some really tough lessons. It's similar to a marriage and divorce where you eventually recognize, "Okay, that relationship didn't work. Let me try another one." It's the same thing with partnerships. Many of them will fall apart over time. Sometimes partnerships run their course because you've had a collaborative partnership for a certain goal. For example, I had one partner where we created a large events company. We decided we would only stay in the state of Arizona and that we would build the business to sell the business. So we created the business, built a big business, put it together, systemized it and then sold the concept of how to do it with a systemized online program. From that, we sold the next thing, which was consulting to sell us, which was to sell our ultimate goal—to sell the business.

So we did that, so that partnership was honest; that partnership was good. It stayed true to what our goal was and then it ran its course. I've been in other partnerships where the other person's core values were not aligned with mine and I think that alignment is really important, that people's core values are aligned to make a partnership work in any way. Because if one person says, "Well I want to do this big project," because they want to became famous, and the other partner says, "because I want to make a difference in lives of people and because I want to do that, I will automatically make money," then the partnership is doomed. One will be very self-centered and one will be very centered to giving back and living their legacy instead of just leaving it for their own fame. I've had both kinds of relationships.

Core values are very important to me. I pay very, very close attention to how people show up. I just had a situation like that. We had a group of seven people who got together—we didn't know each other—in a collaborative project, a big collaborative project. We flew across the country, and had never met before. Even though we had all of these connections through radio shows and e-mails and calls, we were all complete strangers. By the second day, there were six of us that were very well aligned. We had the same core values and the same belief systems even though we came from different backgrounds with different skills sets. One of those people instantly did not fit. That individual was very self-centered and was not a team player. I knew right away in this meeting with these other partners and I just had to call it out. I said, "I can't stay in a group with someone who has such blatantly different core values than I do. I have just left a partnership like that and it will not work, because if it's not aligned, it will be completely out of balance and this whole team will fall apart."

Now, I look at who this potential partner is as a person, because I believe that as we get wiser in business, we want more time, we want more respect of the value that we offer. We are blessed way more in all of those things, but we also feel like when we have had a certain level of success, there is an amount of giving back. There is a feeling that the heart's got to be put into it and, at least for me, it's a very big part. In past partnerships I haven't had that, so it was very important to me to have that heart aligned as well. It took a while to get that person out of the team. Once that person was removed from the team, the collaboration with the other people became even stronger and we're very tight. We are really close and we feel like we've known each other for years and we've only been working on a business project for six months. So, you can you change skills sets, you can give people knowledge, but you can't change who someone is as a person.

John: Well said. Debbie, you do many promotional partnerships and in a promotional partnership, it may not necessarily be a joint venture business collaboration in a traditional sense, but it is a promotional collaboration through an affiliate program or things of that nature where there's reciprocity and mutual benefit. Can you give some examples of how people can work together in collaborating from a promotional perspective?

Debbie: That's exactly where I come from. Joint venture partners are brilliant, and they can move any promotional product faster, whether it's a book, a movie or anything. I've done this from live events. I've had full-time partners where I've gone and travelled and was on the road on a world tour for three years doing a completely collaborative partnership, 100 percent. I have found that it's very challenging for me to do that because that partnership is almost like a marriage. That may not work for most people, so joint venture or collaborative partnerships where you work on individual projects can work better. I have a partner who I work with on live events now. We're very much aligned. Our two programs align beautifully together, we work so great together, but we don't have to be in a business situation together. We get together and do two or three events a year.

Tele-summits or tele-seminars have many joint venture partners in a lot of different fields promoting or sharing our expertise and sharing our databases. Those are very easy to set up and they come from a variety of different connections. They come from people who were featured in books together, people who were in movies together, radio shows, anything. They come from all kinds of things. I briefly mentioned the collaborative partnership we had where we all flew from all over to meet up as complete strangers. That's a collaborative partnership that I have with a group called "Wake Up Women" and we give back, but it's also building a strong business. We are doing a movie together; we're doing events together; we're doing book projects together and we're doing group coaching programs together, but it is completely a joint venture type of partnership that is not a legal contract where we are married to each other in a business. Anyone can walk out at any time if they wanted to, but we are aligned with all the things that we want to create and it's much bigger already than we could have ever imagined.

John: One other thing that needs to be considered that we've talked about earlier and should be reiterated is that even though this is a different type of collaboration, you still need to ensure that there are a few things in place: the person has character and ethics and morals that are in alignment with yours and in addition to that, their target market and their database are also congruent with the type of people you want to reach and need to reach. When people start promoting, cross-promoting, referencing, and giving kudos and credentials and social proof and third-party validations and things of this nature, you need to make sure that the people who are saying how wonderful you are also wonderful themselves, and that the people who will receive this message think that both of you are equally wonderful. The endorsement has to be sincere, and it can only be sincere if there is congruency on all levels—business, ethics, morals, and even within the target market or demographic of the recipient of the message.

Debbie: Most definitely. Then you need to be able to be true to yourself when it isn't right. You need to be able to speak your mind and if you need to walk away because your business reputation is huge, and I know that you pride yourself on that as much as I do. Your reputation is the relationship you have in the business world when you are known worldwide. We are all over the Internet.

When you get a certain level to where your name is out there, whom you align with really becomes even more important, because if you're collaborating with somebody who is doing business unethically or who doesn't have the same type of business respect that you want to have, then you need to speak your mind and move away. It's coming back to that idea of having your goals aligned, your heart centered, and it's also being aware of this business reputation. I will move away from a business relationship if needed because, first, I care about respect and people who will keep that respect in my business relationship. I will walk away from an opportunity to make money any day to save who I am as a person, not only as a person individually, but as a business person. I pride myself on 20-plus years as an expert in this business and for that face that I've never been involved in any bad scams or negativity. Because once you experience that, how do you erase that? Reputation is huge when you're thinking about collaborative partnerships.

John: By the way, what Debbie is speaking about now is called reputation management, and it is something that you need to do for yourself individually, but there are also companies that can provide reputation management and online monitoring services as well. It is something that you can consider looking into further.

Debbie, is there one last bit of wisdom that you can impart to the readers about how to collaborate or why to collaborate? What is your one golden nugget?

Debbie: I feel like you, John. I feel like there's no way we would have the level of success and the experiences and opportunities I have had without so many wonderful collaborations with the right people. It shifts and it changes, and that's okay. Don't stay too long in something that's not working. Always stay true to yourself and what you want and the right people will appear: Powerful and amazing people will appear and when they say, "Come and play," get ready. Put your play clothes on and get out there even if you don't think you are ready, because if somebody believes that you are, it's time to get on board. This has happened to me over and over again. I think when you become that person who somebody has taken onboard so many times and when you have enjoyed the gifts of amazing collaborative partnerships, you just want to give back and help other people have that same experience.

John: Thank you so much, Debbie. I appreciate it.

Debbie: My pleasure.

Debbie Allen is a business and brand strategist, best-selling author and award-winning entrepreneur. Her expertise has been featured in numerous motivational movies including The Opus and The Compass and regularly featured in Entrepreneur Magazine.

Debbie has built and sold numerous million-dollar companies. She mentors clients from around the world on how to become a high-paid expert within their niche market using a step-by-step marketing strategy to develop brand domination. Sign up for Debbie's free marketing course and learn about her upcoming events at www. DebbieAllen.com.

INTERVIEW WITH RYAN LEE

Entrepreneur, Author, Coach and Proud Father of Four

John: I would like to introduce you to my friend and also a coach of mine, Ryan Lee. Ryan and I both started out in the fitness industry many, many years ago. He and I were two of the first fitness entrepreneurs in the world to make a mark online by offering programs, products and services to the fitness industry. Ironically, we both gradually moved into other domains in the business marketing, publishing and public relations fields. Ryan is someone who I can honestly say has changed my life for the better. Although I have had many coaches and people who have influenced my life over the last many years, Ryan is someone who has probably made the most dramatic change and I'm not sure if he's completely aware of that. But with that, welcome Ryan Lee.

Ryan: Thank you, John. I appreciate it.

John: That's why I'm asking you to contribute to this book, because you have skills that I think are very valuable not only to me, but to the readers of this book. What I really I appreciate about what you do is essentially your tag line which is "Success Simplified." That's really what the collaboration economy is all about. Before we get into the specific questions, why "Success Simplified?"

Ryan: I think there's so much great information out there, yet it can be overwhelming. One of my strengths is the ability to get a lot of complex information and just break it down to the simplest parts and make it work more specifically to action sets. The idea of creating a website is overwhelming to people, but if you just go step by step and realize, "Okay, the first thing I have to do is get a domain name. Let's start there." This is exactly how you do it: there's step one, step two, step three, and I simplify the process and then cut out all the nonsense and all of the stuff you don't need and just break it down to the actions you do need. The key is to get people to take action. I think when it's simplified, people will take action.

John: I agree. It's basically chunking and chunking down and if you don't do it correctly, you "up-chunk" it.

Ryan: Many, many times over, correct.

John: So let's get right into this: In today's economy, what are the three best ways—or you can add another one if you like—for business owners and entrepreneurs to collaborate?

Ryan: There are hundreds of ways. One thing I have always said—because I have collaborated a lot over the years and it's something I have learned the hard way—is you must collaborate with people who complement your skill set. For example, in our world of entrepreneurship and online businesses, many of the entrepreneurs tend to be very creative and idea-driven: "Hey, this is a great idea; let's do this; what will create this product?" Those people usually—not always—are not the best finishers—they are not the detail people. They are not the people who are going to spend hours and hours following up with everyone and doing all the project management. What happens is the person who is that go-getter—that energy—goes to an event or a conference or meets someone online. They find someone just like them; same energy, same ideas. They get together and it's great for a while—lots and lots of ideas, lots of energy, lots of new stuff. However, there is no follow through. If you don't follow through, everything starts to sink.

So in the collaboration economy, I think the key before you do anything—before you think of doing any kind of program or product with anyone else—is you have to find someone who complements you. If you are the go-getter, if you're the big idea person who is the visionary, then you need the detailed person. You need the person who is going to sit and write the checks and do the follow-up emails and tackle all the things necessary to grow and to sustain your idea or business. That's huge, John. That's where people drop the ball, and I see so many partnerships fall hard by choosing the wrong people.

John: It's funny, because knowing you and knowing Yanik Silver, we are all very, very similar in this way. When we want something, we don't walk and we don't even run towards it, we dive headfirst and almost attack it. Sometimes that's great, and sometimes it can get us into trouble. Although it is challenging and we have to swallow our pride sometimes, we need people to collaborate with who can reel us back in appropriately to save us from ourselves. Can you give some examples or insight on that?

Ryan: I agree. We own a supplement company and I have partner and cofounder who reels me back in. I'll say, "Do this, do this, do this," and he will respond, "Hold off. Right now, 90 percent of our money is coming from this program. Let's just focus on this for a while." So for me personally, that helps and you need that person to reel you back a little bit, because you can go a little bit overboard.

John: How does that dialogue begin, or can you give some examples of the best way to communicate where each person who is collaborating is heard and respected?

Ryan: Yes, it's a question of just being straight up from the beginning and saying, "Look, we're working together. My strength is being the visionary. My strength is creating the ideas. Your role is to respond to the team, whether I like it or not, and to say, 'Look, that's great. We can look at that later, but let's get this done first,'" and just being real fun about it. In terms of an actual practical tool to use, I have a partner in this one business who likes to use software and spreadsheets to really keep everyone on track. His organization makes sure that there is never any miscommunication. There are no missed emails. All the communication is easy to track. If someone uploads a folder or someone sends something, we can all view it whenever we want or need. All of this organization and detail work really helps our communication, and it helps eliminate a lot the personality things that are always going on, ensuring that there are never any missed phone calls or missed emails. It's like Relationships 101. In any business partnership, you need to be completely up front. A really open and organized approach will help tremendously in relationships and in business partnerships.

I know that some people are hesitant to collaborate, because of fear of being taken advantage of, or being a victim, or somehow missing out on money earned, because of challenges with transparency in accounting and things of that nature. What can someone do when it comes to ensuring transparency? You can say, "I am always honest, and he or she is honest," but how do you really know? What kind of background check do you do? Who do you ask? Who do you rely on to ensure that the people you are collaborating with are who they say they are and will do what they say they will do? That's the great question. I don't do background checks. One great thing about the Internet is that it makes it hard to hide. Step one is you do a Google search, and you do a "deep" Google search. You don't just search for a potential partner once and that's it. You look at his or her name. You add keywords such as refunds, scam and similar terms that might reveal something; obviously, you can't believe everything you see, but if you start seeing a trend coming up over and over again, you will to get an idea of the person you're considering. Everyone now is either going to have a Facebook page, a LinkedIn page or a Twitter account, so look at least one of their social media accounts. See if you have any friends or associates in common and then ask that person, "I'm thinking of working with this person. What do you think? Do you have any insights?" I have done this before with both positive and negative results. You may get great vibes and you may get that bad feeling in your gut that makes you think, "Maybe I shouldn't." If there's even a little hint of that sinking feeling, then don't go ahead with the partnership, because there's very likely some truth to what you hear and what you feel. After you get burned once, you will know how true this is.

John: It's ironic we are having the discussion today about this because just last night, I was asked to contribute or collaborate on a fitness industry product where many top experts were going to do an audio interview on various topics about creating a six-figure income as a fitness professional. This gentleman's selling point to me was to say, "Here are all the other people who are collaborating on this project," and my reply to him was, "That's fantastic. I know all of these people. I respect them and they are my friends." Then I asked him if a couple of other people would be collaborating, because I said based on experience, if they were in, I was out. His reply was these individuals had not been contacted. They would not be participating and that's good because you can have success by association, and you can have guilt or blame by association as well. You have to be conscientious about those things. Then step two for my process will also be to email or call my friends who are on this list of contributors to find out if they have done their portion yet, or what they know about this individual and this project. I think you have to do your due diligence just like you do with any business acquisition or a merger.

Ryan: Absolutely, and you bring up a real good point and that's why I turn down almost all of the programs I'm asked to do. I have been asked to do an interview series and other marketing projects and will always ask, "Who else is doing it?" I look at all the names and can easily say, "Thanks, but no thanks," because I know them. I know their reputation, and I just don't want to be associated with that group. Like you said, it's guilt by association even if you have nothing to do with them. I used to agree to everyone and every interview, instant responding, "Oh, yeah, definitely. I'll help," but I think I was being naïve. I will even turn down well-paying live events that I'm asked to speak at because I'd rather not share the stage with certain people. You do have to be careful. Look around and ask around. If you have that little feeling in your gut that tells you not to do it, then don't do it.

John: How are you collaborating in your business right now? People need to know that you have several business entities across several different platforms and each of them is highly successful and yet, to varying degrees, how are you collaborating? Can you give us some examples of how collaborations are helping your business today to grow?

Ryan: One, I've just finished up recently. I did an online event that is called The Continuity Summit. I've previously done these summits as in-person events. For this fourth one, we decided to try an online event. In terms of collaboration, all the speakers were collaborators. We did interviews right over the Internet. We recorded everything. We streamed captured video and it was 10-12 hours of different experts participating and adding content. That was it. That was literally a collaboration. The entire program was built on collaboration. The experts collaborated with content. They collaborated with the marketing, and with the push. It all worked together. I literally did not have to come up with any new material. The presenters came up with the new material, I asked the questions and I gave them a platform. It was that simple.

John: What about in-person collaboration? How are you collaborating in person? I know you do different coaching and master minds and things like that, but can you give us a specific example?

Ryan: In terms of in-person collaboration, I have a couple of different live things that I do regularly. For speaking engagements and events, I collaborate and bring in guest speakers for specific topics. So if I'm doing a workshop all about marketing or website traffic and I know someone who is in the area who is an expert in the world of Facebook marketing, I'll bring them in and they will collaborate and cover that session. In terms of larger events like multi-day boot camp-type programs, I may have 10, 15 even 20 different speakers, all who contribute different types of content on stage. They are running the show. I am the host and I will usually do my own session. That is the essence of collaboration. I like it because I become the host and resource, I bring in the sponsors and the other presenters, and we all come together in a great collaboration.

John: Yanik Silver calls that creating the platform, which I like. I also would say that you are creating the environment.

Ryan: Yes, it is an environment and, in a way, it is a platform. I look at a platform as a multi-layered thing like a living, breathing organism. With platforms, first you've got your online platforms. Your online platforms can have many different options and outlets. A podcast can be one of your platforms. You can have an online magazine. You can have your email newsletter. You can have your blogs. You can write articles. You can have an online radio show or an online video show. You can have all of these different components of a platform and then you can also have your live thing. You can have your live workshops and live coaching, the live seminars and your boot camps. There are many, many components of a platform, and I am a big believer in developing a large platform, creating different things because there are some people who only want to listen to podcasts or some people who don't want to do any of the online stuff and join membership sites. They only want to go to live in-person events. I think you can offer different learning styles, different collaboration points, and different touch points to different people.

John: It is interesting that you mentioned podcasts, because I am a podcast and iTunes junkie. You, as an individual, can do a podcast and it can be very successful, but there is a clear distinction.

As an individual, you are creating a monologue, which can be dry and boring to some extent in many cases. When you collaborate with other experts, you create real dialogue and interest. When you have this dialogue, it is far easier for the listener to feel that they are participating in a conversation rather than just a monologue, because one is reciprocal and one is unidirectional. The other thing about collaborating in a podcast is that there is no possible way, as smart as you are, that you have all the skills necessary to discuss a wide variety of topics even within your niche, if you do not collaborate. It's an impossibility. Dialogue creates this opportunity.

Ryan: I agree and I think some people try to be everything to everybody, and you can't. You just can't know everything. Take a topic like Facebook, and say, "I'm a Facebook expert." Are you an expert at creating Facebook fan pages or the personal profiles? Are you an expert at buying Facebook ads? If so, what type of ads? You can go so deep on something like Facebook and we're barely even scratching the surface. You just can't know everything. I'm definitely a big fan of collaborating.

John: What is your prediction for the future of business collaboration?

Ryan: I think it is going to continue to increase and continue to grow. More and more business owners and customers are going to expect it and realize that they are going to start getting away from living in the scarcity mentality and start embracing abundance. One of the problems is people often think "The business is about me and if I share the stage with someone, I'm going to be promoting them and it's going to take away from me." The people who get it will succeed. For me, I'm not scared to have an event and host someone who might be seen as a competitor with competing products. I think that, "Hey, this is a person who

I know can help you and I'm going to bring you to them and I'm going to bring them to you." If you get that and you embrace it, it's only going to help your business. The smart business owners know how to collaborate to grow their business. The businesses that are going to continue to grow and embrace abundance will leave the old school who won't do it and who won't check their egos at the door behind.

John: We've talked about collecting in the first part of your life and editing in the second part of your life, where you really refine and figure out who you are and ultimately what you want. For me, I've learned that less is more and less is better: streamlined, automation, elimination, delegation is the way I want to live my life. My wife and I have discovered a love of global travel, and with the technology that is available now, it doesn't even matter, where you're geographically located, unless you need to do something live. Then you need to make sure that everyone is in a compatible time zone, but other than that, there truly are not even any global limitations.

Ryan: This discussion we are having is a perfect example. We don't have to be sitting next to each other. When I did my online continuity program, I had people from all over the world. That limitation is gone.

John: Thanks again. Ryan, do you have any final words of wisdom for the readers who may still be a little reluctant or hesitant to start collaborating?

Ryan: Of course I do. I think if you really want to grow your business, if you truly embrace abundance, you have no choice but to start collaborating. Find people who are going to complement your skills. Find people who you want to be around, who you want to work with, who you think not only could help your business, but you can help their business. Start working with them. Start finding different ways—and I don't mean you have to immediately start a brand-new corporation or a new entity with someone else. It could be something as simple as interviewing each other for your respective websites or giving each other a testimonial. It could be that simple. Start with some simple baby steps and grow the relationships from there. Don't think about starting a year from now or six months from now or even a month from now. Think about starting today and you will be very happy with the results.

Ryan Lee is one of the top marketers in the world. He started his first Internet company in 1998 for less than $100 and has grown it into a full-fledged empire that now brings in seven-figures a month.

He's been featured on the front page of the "Wall Street Journal" and the cover of *Millionaire Blueprints* magazine. Ryan has also written four best-selling books. He was a co-author to the New York Times best-selling series, *The Worst Case Scenario Business Survival Guide*. He reaches more than 300,000 people through his popular site www.ryanlee.com.

INTERVIEW WITH
POLLY BAUER
Credit Expert, Speaker
and Corporate Trainer

Topher: Polly, what do you feel is the biggest difference between working with credit cards todays in the modern world versus say, 20 years ago or maybe even as recent as five years ago?

Polly: There are so many changes. First, the merchants and the consumers are now much more aware of what credit cards cost them in their business; 20 years ago, they were so excited to just be able to accept payments that they really, truly hadn't figured out what the cost of various payments were to them. The difference between accepting a Visa/Mastercard versus accepting an American Express card or accepting a PayPal card versus a private label card, and it's really come top of mind recently when merchants are looking at: How do I increase my bottom line? Where can I cut back some of my expenses? What is it really costing me to accept payments?

Topher: Wow. One of the things that we talk about in the book is that the notion that the new economy is also moving toward private currencies where, for example, I can buy an airplane ticket now using frequent flyer miles. I can buy tickets to the play using my frequent flyer miles and that's literally become a private currency with United Airlines or the airlines. How can a small business owner take advantage of that kind of currency? Is it even possible for a small business to compete with people like that and create their own individual privatized currency to where they could create customers buying with their points or things like that?

Polly: I'm going take a very different stand on points and rewards than most people do. You know that my book covers consumer issues of what it's really costing them to use those types of rewards and are they getting the bang for the buck. When it comes to being a small merchant, it's very difficult to compete with a larger organization. You need to understand that the consumers are realizing there's not a free lunch. They are going back to say, "Are those points costing me more? Carrying more cards in my wallet so I get airline points here and a hotel savings here, what did I really pay for that? Is carrying too many rewards going to driving my credit score down, which is making my insurance payments go up?" So it's a very serious way to look at what can be done. Now, the positive side from a small business owner is if you are still providing the best possible service, you're providing a world-class product, you've got the loyalty people there, there are many things you can do within that organization to keep people continuing to buy. You know, I'm a woman who has got a black belt in shopping, so I buy constantly and I buy with the people that know who I am, what I want, and they're ahead of me in providing the services. So,

I've got like a vigilante team out there of people who let me know when things I like are available and on sale and that's much, much more valuable to me than points on a Discover Card I won't use because when I figured out what those points are really costing me, it's atrocious.

Topher: Wow, interesting. Do you recommend small business owners use gift cards, and do you put that as something different than private currency?

Polly: Yes, gift cards are very different than private currency and I think for a small business owner, having a gift card program can be very successful if they get the right program with the pricing of the cards. You know that the big hopping offerings now is Groupon and Living Social. I've been watching the butcher shop who I buy from constantly through Groupon and they have increased their base price by 25% and I still go in thinking I'm getting a better deal.

Topher: The illusion of the discount.

Polly: Absolutely; what I used to buy for $6.99 is now $11.99, but every time I get that Groupon email to say "your favorite butcher, the guy that carries your lobster tails you love, just spend $40 and I'll give you $80 worth of lobster," I can't resist. But when I come home and do the math, it's like, "Oh, for God's sakes, I fell for this again."

Topher: So with small business owners, then, do you to encourage them or is it a good practice or best practice to take your retail prices and then raise them when you're using a system like Groupon? Because I know a lot of small business owners that refuse to use that because Groupon demands that they get 50% of the discounted price, which leaves more small business owners literally getting pennies on their product versus dollars.

Polly: I don't recommend it. If a merchant's got a great product, a great service and they believe in their product and continually give the consumers what they want—and the key is understanding what the consumers want—then no, they don't need to mark up their prices to be able to have a deal. I recognize that small business owners give the best possible service. They want to know that I want to be a repeat buyer and to me, that makes all of the difference because I'm very, very busy and when they care about me, they pay attention: What do I buy? When do I buy it? How much money do I spend on it? When they recognize me and stay in touch with me and provide something that makes it convenient for me—they have my business hands down.

Topher: One of the things that you shared with me years ago—and it was probably one of the best things—you know how those little gems stay with you for years—was the notion of using American Express or having them as an option. I know a lot of small business owners are reluctant to use American Express simply because they do charge a premium price for that and you don't see as much of a profit when you buy something through American Express. Would you mind sharing with the readers your opinion on American Express and whether or not you should have them as a merchant account?

Polly: I can tell you this—which you and I shared together about seven years ago—I did a cost study analysis for about six months and I tracked the retailers that offered American Express over and above other card products and this is what you have to be aware of:

Who is your client base? If your consumers are business people, if they are taking people to lunch, if they are buying books or supplies for their business, many of their companies will reimburse them on the corporate American Express card, so you don't want to discourage folks in a corporate environment from using that type of product. The survey I shared with you showed that bookstores, retailers and higher ticket item people– whether an air conditioning business or a big print business or somebody who would be buying a year's worth of services—American Express costs 2% more, but they can get a lift in up to 40% on their business buyers. So consumers that use American Express are very loyal and they continue to use American Express and merchants have to look at:

- What is my profit margin?
- What is my cost of goods sold?
- If I had a 42% lift, but I made a little bit less here, would it be worth it to me in sales?

But truly, it all comes down to: Who is my buyer? Is it a stay-at-home mom who may use her Visa? Is it a grandmother who will use her MasterCard, and do I have a whole lot of business buyers? If you've got business buyers, it's worth the difference for American Express.

Topher: Is it legal to offer better pricing for using different credit cards? So, if I wanted to, could I give people who use American Express an extra $5 off of my product even though I know I'd lose more, but give me that bump, knowing that that just pre-qualifies them to be a better customer because they have an American Express card. Is that something you would recommend, or is that even legal?

Polly: Until recently, it could not be done. However, regulations changed so that the merchant can now be honest with the consumer and say, "Mrs. Smith, I pay more on American Express. Would you mind putting this product on your Visa card? Do you have a Visa or MasterCard? " They can be very honest. They weren't allowed to share that in the past but merchants can drive whatever card is their card of preference. They can also ask the consumer for a different card, which was always a violation for up to 30 years. Now it is legal. They can communicate to the consumer that it costs a little bit more for that card and tell the consumer, "I want to keep my prices down," and—this is the big caveat—as of October 2012, merchants can now either give a discount for a specific card, they can encourage a particular card's use, and they can say, "We are a MasterCard shop and we prefer MasterCard." Those regulations have been in place for 34 years and have just been recently changed. So yes, the merchant now has control of:

- what type of products he wants to offer; and also
- what type of card plastics he wants the consumer to buy on.

Now, I would be reluctant if I didn't share the newest regulation. For years it did not make a difference whether someone bought from you on a debit card or a credit card. It was all blended in their discount rate. That is no longer true thanks to the Durbin Act and the Dodd-Frank Act. If a merchant can ask their consumers for a debit transaction, it cuts their costs; it can cut the cost as much as 2% on that transaction. Now, if you're an Internet merchant, obviously, you don't have the PIN pad's capability of taking that debit card product, but when you are in a retail store, the cost savings for a retailer can be massive by taking the debit card. It's critical that small business owners understand the importance of driving customers to debit when possible; if it's a large-ticket item, that will be hard, but for heaven's sakes, save the cost. Save the price of that transaction. Two percent (sometimes it's a little over 1%; sometimes it's as high as 2%) could be a tremendous savings to the bottom line.

Topher: Great. Polly, thank you so much. For those of you who have not yet enjoyed Polly's book, "*The Plastic Effect*," I think it is an absolute must-read for any small business owner who uses merchant card transactions. And if you're reading this book, you'd better be using merchant services. It is absolutely a treasure chest full of great information in terms of the psychology behind how people buy, why they buy, and how you can use merchant services and credit cards with your business intelligently.

Polly, thank you very much. I appreciate your time.

Polly: "*The Plastic Effect*" is written for consumers about how to manage money, how to keep credit scores high. With the average household having $15,488 in revolving credit and debt right now, that is why "*The Plastic Effect*" was created for the consumer. The second book is "*The Credit Intelligence.*" That's written for merchants.

Polly A. Bauer, CPCS, CME is widely known today as "the credibility queen" in business and communications. During the past 40 years as a corporate CEO, board member, industry association leader, consultant, advisor and corporate speaker, Polly has shown organizations and individuals how to rise to the top through credibility in communications.

Polly followed her passion in the credit card industry from her youth to President and CEO of the Home Shopping Network Credit

Corporation. Along the way, she managed a $950 million credit card portfolio, consulted with the leading global financial service companies, supported industry policy development, created industry standard systems and practices, and helped numerous businesses to avert fraud.

Polly knows credibility in communication as a business leader. CEO of Polly Bauer & Associates, a corporate speaking and consulting firm, Polly speaks before 25 or more corporations, professional associations and women's organizations each year. She is one of a select few to achieve the highest level in the professional speaking industry, the Master Corporate Speaker Certification. Clients and audiences alike characterize Polly as high energy, entertaining, inspiring and action-oriented.

www.speakerpollybauer.com

INTERVIEW WITH KEVIN HARRINGTON
Productization

Topher: Kevin, you've been in business for more than 30 years. What is the biggest difference between how you do your business today versus how you did it 30 years ago?

Kevin: There is a big difference in how I do business today because we didn't have the Internet 30 years ago. Thirty years ago, you came out with a product, and it could last two years, three years, or five years before you had any kind of significant awareness around the world. Now we launch a product and, almost instantly, everyone in the world sees that product. So people follow us in Japan, in Korea, in Germany, and they're following the trends of the marketers in the United States instantly, so we have to protect ourselves. We have more strenuous legal protection, patent protection and ways to test products so we don't put them out to the masses.

Topher: What is one of those techniques?

Kevin: We can talk about some of it, but the bottom line is, in the old days we would shoot a show, test it, and that might cost $100,000—$200,000. Now, we can go on the Internet and we can do web tests. So we use a mailing list, an email list of a million buyers, and we throw it out to those people, then we rank it 1 to 10 in performance. Because we've got a history of successful products that have been launched, we now know if something does a 2 on a scale of 1 to 10, we don't want to mess with that product. If it does a 7, 8 or a 9, then it warrants more analysis as to whether we want to invest in it.

Topher: What do you think makes an idea or a product a 7, 8 or a 9? Every entrepreneur thinks that their idea is a million-dollar idea right? Every idea is a winner until you put it into test.

Kevin: A product or an idea should solve a problem such that there's nothing already in the marketplace that's solving it in a similar fashion. So sometimes that's very difficult to find that, but if you can solve that problem in a unique fashion, you may have a home run. But I also look for something that has some kind of magical transformation. If you're in the business of getting people out of debt, the magical transformation is you're owed a lot of money and now you don't owe a lot of money.

Or helping people improve their credit, you had bad credit, now you have good credit. If it's losing weight, here you are 200 pounds, now you're 120 pounds. Or if you had acne and now you have a clear-skinned face, that magical transformation is very visual and very demonstrable. So those are all things that seek out.

Topher: So an entrepreneur should, no matter what their product or service, ask themselves, "What is my magical transformation I provide?"

Kevin: Correct.

Topher: Now, you talked about the old way of doing business. It could take years to get something to the market, now it's literally a matter of months to get something to market. Do you feel that because of that, there's a decline in quality because obviously, if you have two years to do something, you can perfect it. I always say that one of the biggest troubles for an entrepreneur today is perfectionism because they will sit on a brilliant idea and perfect it. By the time they perfect it; somebody else already solved it. iPhones are a great example. They're far from perfect. They just get it out to market. What would you advise an entrepreneur today in regard to getting their idea or product out, what's a reasonable time? What is a reasonable success rate? Is there anything that you can sit there and go, "Look, 80% is good. 60% is good." Is there a percentage?

Kevin: First, the amount of time it takes to bring a product out depends on so many variables, and if you're looking at just the product world that I'm in, if it's electrical or if it's ingestible, you've got studies and electrical tasks and UL requirements. Those can take six months, a year or longer even so that adds to the time to bring a product out to the market.

If it's just a blasted injection moulded product, you might be able to bring it out in 90 or 120 days. The one thing that I suggest is if you're going to take something out to the masses, it needs to be at 90-plus% because somebody else is going to see this, knock it off, and make it 90-plus%, and they're going to sell 10 million and this guy is going to sell 10,000. Do not launch until you get that next 10% and that's only going to take another 60 days. However, these people are very anxious and they want to go, so, I'm going to walk from the deal if they want to do this because I need to take this to the next step. They may go out and test it and be successful with it, which I think they will be, but they haven't perfected it yet. I suggest undercover testing as we discussed **before, so that they're not alerting the market to what they've got if it is something very unique.**

Topher: So in today's modern culture of get it out fast, get it out quick, you're almost saying, slow down a bit. Don't be seduced by technology.

Kevin: Exactly. Three years ago, we would launch something and within 30 days there would be 100 competitors on the Internet. If we do things properly now and we get something tested before anybody knows, then when we launch, we've got 100 websites of our own that are out there before the others become the first 100 websites to knock us off. We become our own knock-off before we let anybody else. So then when people come in and they see what's going on, they say, "Oh, there's already too much of it out there." So we can keep our competitors away by knocking ourselves off. That only happens if we test properly under the radar.

Topher: I always say that we live in a plug and play world. You don't have to pay people to customize anything online because there are so many templates out there. Are there services that an entrepreneur can use to test something? Are there services that test under the radar?

Kevin: These are proprietary. I use them for all of my products and relationships but we don't like to tell the world who they are but it's not a service that we own. We use a company that does this and it's spending years in the business and losing a lot of money on tests that have given us the access to these kinds of companies but yes, they are definitely out there. Anybody who wants to find out about can contact me directly and we'll work it out.

Topher: This book is called "*Collaboration Economy.*" It's about coming up with the new entrepreneurs' attitude that there is no level of scarcity out there. That doesn't mean you shouldn't be competitive but we don't want to stick people as competitors or something like that. What advice would you give people who are still in that old school mentality of, "These are my competitors. I'm not going to open up my IP to them and I'm going to keep things secret." I understand that you've got to keep things protected; I get that. Do you have examples or experiences in your life where competition didn't work but collaboration did?

Kevin: Yes, I believe in collaboration. Industries get very competitive, but I like partnering with people in our industry. I have a particular strength and it's in hard goods such as fitness products, housewares products, hardware products. Guthy Renker is a competitor of mine. They have a particular expertise in beauty products, more soft creams, lotions, potions, acne, and beauty—that kind of thing. Then there's another competitor, BeachBody that is very strong in the DVD and IP marketplace. So, I've referred projects on a venture basis to both companies and I've collaborated with them. Guthy Renker and I have formed ventures where we take some of our products that fit more of their mould and their products that fit more of our mould and we venture together because we have strengths in our particular arenas. So I believe that when you venture with your partner, you end up learning some of their strengths and some of their operational sides. Guthy Renker is very tight on continuity because beauty is about buying one and shipping it for eight more months. We've picked up continuity techniques by collaborating with them on our hard goods side of the business to be able to get extra revenues out of people who only would buy one juicer but maybe there is a continuity of vitamins we can send them because we know have opened our minds after these collaborations and these partnering ventures. So, I believe partnering is very good. Also, anytime you're in a friendly competitive environment, it makes for a more fun environment also.

Topher: It forces you to raise your game a little bit as well.

Kevin: Absolutely.

Topher: What do you see in the future of entrepreneurship? Where do you think we're heading for the next five to 10 years, and are there any trends that you can see?

Kevin: As many companies have difficult times, there are going to be plenty of lay-offs. Plenty of people used to work in companies for 20 years, 30 years and 40 years. In many cases, it is now less than three years. So if people are turning their jobs much more rapidly, that means they're unemployed more often and when they're unemployed, they need extra income and that's when the entrepreneurship kicks in. I believe the world of entrepreneurship is ever increasing and by the way, being an entrepreneur doesn't mean you have to quit your job and go full time.

There are many weekend-warrior entrepreneurs and I believe that that is a huge trend that is going to grow much more rapidly over the next number of years because people in transition have hundreds of business opportunities that could help them make more income than they could have been making from their job.

Topher: So the time to become an entrepreneur is when you're an employee, not when you're unemployed?

Kevin: Absolutely. There are lots of people making 20-30% extra income just by working a day or two a week in the evenings and on the weekends and that's nice little supplemental income. Then if you then get a notice that you're going to be unemployed, you have this little business that you can kick into high gear and you've got yourself a full-time business.

Topher: Thank you very much Kevin.

Kevin: My pleasure.

Kevin Harrington is widely acknowledged as a pioneer and principal architect of the infomercial industry. In 1984, Kevin produced one of the industry's first 30-minute infomercials. Since then, he has been involved with more than 500 product launches that resulted in sales of more than $4 billion worldwide with 20 products that reached individual sales of more than $100 million.

Kevin founded Quantum International, Ltd. in the mid-1980s, which merged into National Media Corporation in 1991. Under his leadership as President, National Media reached $500 million in annual sales distributing in more than 100 countries and 20 languages. This company's success has been chronicled in a case study at Harvard/MIT for more than a decade. Kevin was also selected as an investor "Shark" on the ABC television series "Shark Tank."

www.kevinharrington.tv

CONCLUSION

Are you ready to collaborate in the new economy?

If so, get ready for a wonderful ride.

Collaboration is all about partnerships and connecting with the right people. It's all about dynamic business planning, branding and working within a carefully thought-out micro-niche. It's all about recognizing the difference between the old economy and the new economy.

The following 10 steps will provide a great checklist for your ongoing efforts to collaborate in today's economy:

1. Find your micro-niche and truly own it.
2. Remember that yesterday's competition is today's ally: Determine your best allies.
3. Focus on creating frictionless transactions.

4. Be willing to give away seven hours of your best content for free before you gain traction with paying customers.

5. Become a celebrity within your micro-niche. Focus on publishing and getting recognized within your industry.

6. Take advantage of the myriad affiliate marketing opportunities available online today.

7. Take control of your personal brand and your business brand.

8. Remember that friends are more reliable than the Internet.

9. Focus on becoming a Key Person of Influence in your industry even more than simply running your business. Once you're recognized as a KPI, the business will flow much easier.

10. Consider how you can use private currency within your business to make transactions easier than ever for customers.

These 10 simple and effective tips will help get your small business off the ground and soaring into the stratosphere as you engage in the new collaborative economy of business success.

YOUR RESOURCE LIST

The following resources will provide further information on the topics covered in "Collaboration Economy:"

Official Collaboration Economy website:
    www.collaborationeconomy.com
Topher Morrison: www.tophermorrison.com
John Spencer Ellis: www.johnspencerellis.com
Yanik Silver: www.surefiremarketing.com
Debbie Allen: www.debbieallen.com
Ryan Lee: www.ryanlee.com
Polly Bauer: www.speakerpollybauer.com
Kevin Harrington: www.kevinharrington.tv
TravelTrep: Blog, community and resources to help you become a
    traveling entrepreneur and live a life of adventure:
    www.traveltrep.com
Learn how to become a Key Person of Influence:
    www.keypersonofinfluence.com/usa/

Get just about anything done for $5: www.fiverr.com

Hire talented people to write code, edit, write press releases, and build almost anything and much more on Elance: www.elance.com

Hire My Mom provides talented, experienced professionals in a variety of fields including: administrative, research, writing, graphic design, editing, accounting, web design, customer service, virtual assisting, coaching, sales, marketing, public relations, bookkeeping, legal, desktop publishing, creative arts, medical billing, ecommerce, strategic planning, database development, payroll, human resources, etc. www.hiremymom.com

"Entrepreneur Revolution" by Daniel Priestley

"Free" by Chris Anderson

"Zero Moment of Truth" by Jim Lecinski

"The Brand Called You: The Ultimate Personal Branding Handbook to Transform Anyone into an Indispensable Brand" by Peter Montoya and Tim Vandehey

"The Personal Branding Phenomenon: Realize greater influence, explosive income growth and rapid career advancement by applying the branding techniques of Michael, Martha and Oprah" by Peter Montoya

ABOUT THE AUTHORS

Topher Morrison:

Topher Morrison is Managing Director of Entrevo USA, a growth accelerator firm based in Tampa, Florida, which has worked with more than 1,000 companies globally in helping them to dominate their market share. His extensive speaking schedule spanning the past 25 years has taken him throughout the United States, UK, Australia and Singapore and earned him a global reputation as an expert in mass communications and influence. Topher has spoken for top execs with American Express, Microsoft and Google, just to name a few.

In addition, Topher is the author of the best-selling book, *"Stop Chasing Perfection and SETTLE FOR EXCELLENCE,"*—

which has been hailed as "the self-help book for people who are sick of self-help books."

In contrast to most professional speakers, Topher's shockingly honest, sometimes irreverent and always down-to-earth approach is surprisingly infectious. His personality and straightforward manner is perfect for people who are tired of fleeting success in "self-help sinkholes." He is not afraid to tell it like it is and shatter the myth of achieving overnight success. Instead, Topher speaks to the savvy businessperson who could care less about motivational "magic wands" and is more focused on getting tangible, proven strategies to become a key person of influence in their company, network, or industry.

Contact Topher at www.tophermorrison.com

John Spencer Ellis:

John splits his time living in Las Vegas, Southern California and traveling the world. He has helped create over 500,000 jobs globally. Each week, more than one million people enjoy a fitness and personal development program he's created. John is the CEO of the National Exercise & Sports Trainers Association (NESTA), Spencer Institute for Life Coaching, International Triathlon Coaching Association (ITCA) and the Mixed Martial Arts Conditioning Association (MMACA).

NESTA is the parent of Wexford University, which offers associate through doctoral degrees in fitness, nutrition and sport psychology. John created Adventure Boot Camp, the world's largest fitness boot camp system, as well as Intense Mixed Performance Accelerated Cross Training (IMPACT), Kung-fu Fitness and TACTIX. He developed programs used by Cirque du Soleil, the U.S. Army, Navy, Air Force, Marines, and Coast Guard. He consults the Ultimate Fighting Championships (UFC).

John is an Amazon #1 Best-selling Author, award-winning filmmaker and international speaker. He holds degrees in business, marketing, health promotion and education.

Contact John at www.johnspencerellis.com